The Art of SERIES
EDITED BY CHARLES BAXTER

T0016274

The Art of series is a line of books reinvigorating the practice of craft and criticism. Each book is a brief, witty, and useful exploration of fiction, nonfiction, or poetry by a writer impassioned by a singular craft issue. *The Art of* volumes provide a series of sustained examinations of key, but sometimes neglected, aspects of creative writing by some of contemporary literature's finest practitioners.

THE ART OF REVISION

THE LAST WORD

Also by Peter Ho Davies

The Art of

REVISION

THE LAST WORD

Peter Ho Davies

Graywolf Press

"I Remember, I Remember" from *The Less Deceived* by Philip Larkin used with permission from Faber and Faber Ltd.

This publication is made possible, in part, by the voters of Minnesota through a Minnesota State Arts Board Operating Support grant, thanks to a legislative appropriation from the arts and cultural heritage fund. Significant support has also been provided by Target Foundation, the McKnight Foundation, the Lannan Foundation, the Amazon Literary Partnership, and other generous contributions from foundations, corporations, and individuals. To these organizations and individuals we offer our heartfelt thanks.

MINNESOTA
STATE ARTS BOARD

CLEAN
WATER
LAND &
LEGACY
AMENDMENT

Published by Graywolf Press
250 Third Avenue North, Suite 600
Minneapolis, Minnesota 55401

All rights reserved.

www.graywolfpress.org

Published in the United States of America

ISBN 978-1-64445-039-0

2 4 6 8 9 7 5 3 1
First Graywolf Printing, 2021

Library of Congress Control Number: 2020951356

Cover design: Scott Sorenson

For
Thomas Einion Davies
1934–2018

*—You know what question really drives me
insane . . . and it happens every goddamned time:
"How do you know when it's finished?"*

—Well, sometimes it's hard to tell . . .

*—She's talking about a Jackson Pollock we saw at
a gallery.*

—Yeah. Why not three splatters less, or two more?

*—That's what makes Pollock Pollock, right? He can
just stare at it and say: "That's it. It's complete.
It's finished." That's what makes you an artist.*

—*Billions,* season 5, episode 7: "The Limitless Shit"
by Emily Hornsby, Brian Koppelman, and David Levien

Contents

THE ART OF REVISION

THE LAST WORD

Prologue: A Study of Provincial Life

Here is a story: it happens to be true.

In 1979, when I was twelve or thirteen—around the same age as my own son as I write this—I witnessed an act of heroism on my father's part. Not "everyday" heroism of the working-a-job-he-hated-to-support-his-family variety, or the faithful-to-his-wife-for-fifty-years variety, or even the regular-visits-to-his-aged-mother-in-a-nursing-home variety (though he practiced all of those, too), but old-school, stand-up, risking-physical-harm-for-the-sake-of-another heroism.

This was in my hometown of Coventry, England—the model for George Eliot's *Middlemarch*; I'm borrowing her subtitle for this vignette—a Saturday morning on a busy downtown shopping street. Through the crowds we saw a boy—a teenager, maybe sixteen or seventeen—running toward us. We probably heard him first, his footsteps echoing off the concrete and plate glass. Except he wasn't just running, I thought, he was running a race. Leading three or four others. Except they weren't racing him, I realized, they were *chasing* him. And they were skinheads. And he was wearing a turban. This at a time when the far-right National Front was resurgent in Britain.

But even as I registered these details, I couldn't make sense of them in the moment, clinging to my first impression that it might all have been some lark, teenage high jinks. Even when the chasers caught up with the chased, knocked him down, put the boot in, I don't think I fully understood what was happening. Nor, I'm sure, did the other shoppers around us. I like to think they didn't intervene, not out of fear for themselves— there was no time for that rationalization—but out of simple shock and incomprehension.

In fact, my father was the only one to go to that boy's aid, pushing and pulling the attackers off him. Luckily, as bullies will, they ran off as soon as confronted. Luckily, their victim wasn't too badly injured, physically at least. After picking himself up and dusting himself off he thanked my father, but refused further help (in the quintessentially British form of the offer of a cup of tea) and hastily limped off in the other direction.

The whole thing took less than five minutes. The crowd of Saturday shoppers began to flow again, and after a moment my father and I merged with it. I don't even recall much talking about the incident with him. But I've never forgotten it.

Here is a revision of that story, a version of it that I told near the start of my 2007 novel, *The Welsh Girl*, transposed to 1930s Germany and told from the point of view of a German Jew, called Rotheram (the Anglicized version of "Roth" that he eventually adopts), grappling with the decision to emigrate:

> He'd been dead set against leaving, even after seeing a fellow beaten in the street. It had happened so fast: the slap of running feet, a man rounding the corner, hand on his hat, chased by three others. Rotheram had no idea what was going on even as the boots went in, and then it was over, the thugs charging off, their victim curled on the wet cobbles. It was a busy street and no one moved, just watched the man roll onto one knee, pause for a moment, taking stock of his injuries, then pull himself to his feet and limp hurriedly away, not looking at any of them. *As if ashamed*, Rotheram thought. He'd barely realized what was happening, yet he felt as if he'd failed. Not a test of courage, not that, he told himself, but a test of comprehension. He felt stupid standing there gawking like all the rest. Too slow on the uptake to have time to fear for himself. When he told his mother, she clutched his hand and made him promise not to get involved in such things. He shook her off in disgust, repeated that he hadn't been afraid, but she told him sharply, "You should have been."

So, a story and its revision: a pairing that I'd like to use to consider the nature of revision.

I'll revisit this specific example in more detail later, but for now I just want to ask the basic question: What's changed?

The setting, the context, most obviously. The place and time, as I described in my preamble to each version, and the attendant details (one victim wears a hat, the other a turban).

But also, we might note, the action has changed—the thugs *choose* to run off, rather than *being* run off. The characters, too—notably, there's no hero, no figure equivalent to my father. Plus, the attack in Germany is observed by a somewhat older point-of-view figure—Rotheram is a young man suspended somewhere between my childhood and my father's adulthood at the time of the original incident.

We could pursue this catalog of changes further, of course, down to the level of individual word choices: the "echoing" footsteps in the first version versus the "slap of running feet" in the second, say, two descriptions of the same sound, one hinting at the reverberations of memory, the other a foreshadowing of violence.

And yet, for all these myriad changes it's also worth noting how much of the initial story, its basic terms, remains. It's still *recognizably* the same event, down to its details, which is how we know it's a revision. There's a hint here of the underlying writerly anxiety about revision: the confounding uncertainty of how much to change. Too much? Not enough? Any writer who's ever despaired that revision seems endless, or feared that they might ruin their work with one more change, or been caught paralyzed between the two, will know what I mean.

The question I want to pose then in this book is: What do all these changes amount to? What do they add up to, even as our drafts remain recognizably related? And, (how) is the resultant whole greater than the sum of its altered parts? Which is to say, *What is revision?* Call it, for now, the sum of what changes, and what stays the same, and the alchemical reaction between them.

Black Box

Describing what revision is turns out to be a surprisingly tricky proposition. That's partly because describing *any* change is problematic. How to pin down a process in flux? In biology the answer is evolution. In math—my father was an engineer, and for a while we both thought I'd follow in his footsteps—the answer is calculus . . . which just goes to give an idea of the challenge!

Fortunately, literature has its own mechanism for describing change. So while I might resort to a long list of tips and tactics to delineate revision, I'd like instead to reach for a more engaging structure. And as a fiction writer, the natural organization I incline to, literature's theory of change, is narrative, story. Revision, after all, is the journey of a story—the *story* of a story, if you like—and of its writer's relationship with that story. As such—like any journey, like any story—it has a beginning, a middle, and an end.

The beginning of revision, appropriately enough, is vision. Yet *seeing* revision is easier said than done.

As a teacher of writing, I've often been struck by the sense that revision is an overlooked, underaddressed, even invisible aspect of our work: the "elephant in the workshop," if you will. It's notionally what most of our discussion in fiction classes, or constructive feedback from any trusted reader, points toward. Ideally, the value—the lessons, the suggestions, the encouragement and energy—of such feedback extends into revision of the stories shared. But while a typical manuscript critique will raise issues about a draft and discuss possible remedies, the revisions resulting from those discussions are themselves likely to remain invisible to most of us. That's inevitable when individual classes come together relatively briefly, but even students I work with in an MFA program may only share a couple drafts of a story over two years, and then not always with the same readers. The upshot is that for all the work we share, we don't get to see very much of one another's revision process.

This isn't just a function of creative writing teaching. Revision has historically been hidden away from the view of all but a select few readers—editors mostly. To be sure, writers often talk about revision in interviews, but rarely with complete candor. Even when such comments aren't touched by humble-bragging or hindsight bias, they're likely to be limited for fear of spoilers or of overexplaining a book. Readers certainly don't typically have direct access to multiple drafts of published work.

There are a few exceptions to this: early drafts of *The Great Gatsby*, and *Lady Chatterley's Lover*, brought to light and published largely as a result of scholarly interest, or rare reissues of books like Stephen King's "complete and uncut" edition of *The Stand* or Peter Matthiessen's "new rendering" of his Watson trilogy in *Shadow Country*. These feel like the literary equivalent of DVD extras or director's cuts of cult movies. The 2015 publication of Harper Lee's *Go Set a Watchman*, billed as a follow-up to *To Kill a Mockingbird* but now understood as an earlier draft of that classic, is a more recent example, albeit the initial description of it as a sequel is another instance of the cultural obfuscation of revision.

Most of us never get to trace the genesis of any work other than our own, which seems strange and a little problematic given that in most every other aspect of our craft, writers are encouraged to learn from other writers by reading and studying their work. In that fashion, we might learn enhanced dialogue skills from one writer, better plotting from another, techniques for how to move in and out of flashback from a third. And to be sure, we often deploy such skills in later drafts of the revision process. But are they the entirety of revision?

Benjamin Percy makes a productive distinction between revision for novice and for experienced writers:

"When revising, the beginning writer spends hours consulting the thesaurus, replacing a period with a semicolon, cutting adjectives, adding a few descriptive sentences—whereas the professional writer mercilessly lops off limbs, rips out innards like party streamers, drains away gallons of blood, and then calls down the lightning to bring the body back to life."

We might list a catalog of things most of us needed to learn when we were beginners—avoiding the tic-y repetitions of certain words, the reliance on cliché, the overuse of adverbs, and so forth. Many of these small elements of style have to be learned, which is to say that for most of us they are at some point a feature of revision. The same is true for aspects of technique. When I was starting out, for instance, I didn't include much dialogue in my stories (young writers have a common tendency to get "stuck" in a mode—telling or showing) and had to remind myself to incorporate scenes during revision. But that hasn't been true for a long time now; the toggling between modes of scene and narration has become more intuitive, natural even, as I've become more practiced. Which is to say that, like Benjamin Percy's, my experience of revision has altered over time, as I've revised myself as a writer, so much so that many of those hard-learned skills have become second nature, showing up even in first drafts. This is good news, of course, but it also suggests that revision is a moving target. Experienced writers still wrestle with revision, but such is the protean nature of the process that it's not the same revision as earlier in their careers. And what's fundamental to revision, I'd suggest, is not what the beginning writer does, but what the experienced writer does. Theoretically, I suppose, there might be an infallible writer, one who—with enough experience—writes perfect first drafts, but I doubt it. Even God needed to start over after the Flood (and apparently still felt the need for a sequel . . .). So what does it mean when a writer who has mastered all the technical skills still needs to revise? What's that final irreducible core of revision? What's left to change?

The lists of revision tips (however useful) that feature in many articles and manuals about writing, then, would seem to not tell the whole story. We begin to intuit that revision isn't just a catchall description for the various refinements of craft, but a skill in itself, a technique of its own, a state of mind even. In which case the paucity of its examples might limit our insight. Eliot's (or Wilde's or Picasso's) famous dictum "good writers borrow, great writers steal" is, after all, a distinction without a difference if the prize—revision, in this case—is secure in some impenetrable vault.

We might, in passing, compare this state of affairs to the practices in other arts. Painters, say, leave us sketches, studies, cartoons (often prized as works of art in their own right). Many gallery shows contain *series* of works, variations on a theme, which differ only slightly from one another and might (loosely) be imagined as a set of drafts. And compared to the black box of literary revision, a rehearsal process—in the dramatic arts or music—is an open book. Stand-up comedians provide yet another example of public revision. Their bits and sets are often developed in clubs, on the circuit, over time—weeks and months, if not years—in front of live audiences. For the comic these performances are in a sense drafts—jokes are honed, added, deleted. Audiences are typically asked not to record these drafts, though the acts of certain celebrated (and/or infamous) comics are sometimes reviewed multiple times by critics as they're performed in small clubs, on tour, and finally in TV specials.

The invisibility of revision in fiction is, of course, my excuse for talking about my own experiences of it. In truth, much of my teaching and most of my craft knowledge derive in some sense from my own work (it may be the only thing I'm truly expert in), but in the case of revision the choice seems apt for another reason. Revision is very much a process of close reading ourselves and our work. As such, this book, like the anecdote it begins with, is a personal story of revision, though one I hope individual readers will call upon their own experiences of writing and reading to extend, adapt, and indeed revise.

There are to be sure a handful of notable instances of published drafts that we might draw on. The textbook pairing—fitting given his own avowal that "it's instructive, and heartening both, to look at the early drafts of great writers"—is a couple of Raymond Carver stories: "The Bath" and "A Small, Good Thing." And yet the utility of those famous examples is complicated by what we now know: that these are less instances of revision by Carver than of far-reaching cuts and changes by his editor Gordon Lish, which Carver himself felt deeply equivocal about. Fascinating and instructive as the competing versions of these stories are, the revision process can once again be obscured if it's too tightly conflated with the editorial process.

Over the years, I've collected several other instances in which two drafts of the same story have been published. The Irish writer Frank O'Connor published multiple versions of the same story during his long career. The other O'Connor, Flannery, revisited her first published story, "The Geranium," at the end of her career in a fascinating and convoluted recapitulation entitled "Judgement Day." The collected stories of Isaac Babel similarly contain another pair of published drafts in the stories "My First Fee" and the earlier "Information." More recently, several of Wells Tower's stories in his collection *Everything Ravaged, Everything Burned* illustrate the sometimes radical changes between the version of a story originally published in a literary journal and the version collected in a book. The telltale phrase "some of these stories previously appeared in different form in the following journals" can be found in the acknowledgments of many short story collections, including my own, but Tower is unique in that different versions of his story "Retreat" appear in two issues of the same journal, *McSweeney's*. Lately, in an encouraging development, a new magazine, *Draft: The Journal of Process*, has begun publishing fascinating early versions of stories, including Carmen Maria Machado's "The Husband Stitch."

I'll consider several of these examples in more detail as we move on, and all of them are worth seeking out, but it's noticeable that they *have* to be sought out. They have an air of the scholarly, the obscure, the collector's item that seems contrary to the inevitable ubiquity of revision. Their very rarity is part of the problem. They make what should be the norm seem exceptional. Furthermore, even these examples, instructive as they are, are only snapshots of an ongoing process. Work in progress is after all work in motion, a single draft no more than a freeze frame.

These curios and the corresponding frequency with which the same few Carver examples crop up in classes and textbooks—I still teach them myself—illustrate the invisibility of revision, but what's really at issue is the corollary of that invisibility: the misunderstand-

ing of what revision is, and—like all invisible labor—
the underappreciation of it.

I've generally felt fortunate, over twenty-some years
of teaching, that creative writing is a pretty "cool" subject for undergraduates (it's arguable the competition
isn't too stiff). The students tend to want to be in the
class, and are usually willing to do the work. In my experience, however, revision is the exception—the perenni-
ally "uncool" aspect of creative writing that undergrads,
but also a few graduate students, still resist.

When I ask students to revise their stories, the
results—even from talented writers—are often under-
whelming. I get dutiful drafts wherein the students half-
heartedly take two or three suggestions from workshop,
making just enough mechanical changes to begrudg-
ingly acknowledge the feedback. This is revision as
grade grubbing. Alternatively, I get "drafts" so wholly
unrecognizable from their originals—not so much the
baby thrown out with the bathwater as baby, bathwater,
rubber ducky, and all thrown out *in* the bathtub for
convenience—that they're essentially brand-new first
drafts. Writing researchers designate these students, respectively, as "recopiers" and "restarters."

Both these responses are less revisions per se than
rejections of revision. The first somewhat arrogantly
implies *My story doesn't really need any improvement*;
the second rather abjectly suggests *My story is so bad,*

so hopelessly beyond repair, I can't bear to look at it again, so I'll start over.

I don't mean to suggest that all aspiring writers share these inexperienced attitudes to revision. Though, since all writers, myself included, swing from arrogance to abjection, often in the same morning, we might recognize something of ourselves in these callow responses. And even if you've overcome the resistance to revision that my undergrads are struggling with, even if you're now a self-professed "lover of revision," if you've ever plaintively asked "How many drafts is enough? How do I know when a story is done?" you likely share some of their underlying anxiety and resentment about revision. An anxiety that is as much about how to do it, as what it is.

Let's start with what it's not.

My undergraduates, I've come to realize, are struggling with a bias—ingrained and likely unconscious—against revision.

Revision in high school or middle school can easily and narrowly seem to mean *grammatical* revision. Valuable as those lessons are, they tend to make revision feel like a chore, about as much fun as tidying one's room, or "washing the dishes," as Colson Whitehead puts it. ("Revision" in Britain when I was in school also had the additional unfortunate connotation of "revising for an exam"—rote learning, or cramming, in other words.) The danger is that in this limited sense revision comes to seem rigid, rule-based, *proper*—the antithesis of everything "cool" about creativity. (Tidying one's room, after all, has a known—boring—outcome, though consider if your mom told you there was treasure hidden somewhere in that mess. Suddenly the tidying is allied to a potential of discovery, which feels a little closer to the truth of revision.)

Certain widely taught regimented communications practices of the "Tell 'em what you're going to say; *say* it; then tell 'em what you've said" variety (originally a strategy for sermons) or the five-paragraph essay probably share a portion of blame here. But there are other even deeper cultural forces lined up against revision, and in favor of first drafts.

There's our tendency, say, to romanticize inspiration over perspiration, to consider the first draft the best draft. The popular image of certain writers might factor in here—think Jack Kerouac composing *On the Road* on that continuous roll of paper. Truman Capote's famously withering response, "That's not writing, that's typing," is worth recalling, and yet Kerouac's 120-foot "scroll" (a single paragraph, single spaced; Kerouac could type a Benzedrine-assisted 100 words a minute) continues to have an iconic status in the cultural imagination. My son had seen it on display no less than three times before he was thirteen, at the Pompidou Center in Paris, the British Library, and the American Writers Museum in Chicago. The truth is that Kerouac *did* in fact revise. Despite his editor Robert Giroux's plaintive "But Jack, how can you make corrections on a manuscript like that?" there's evidence of as many as six drafts composed in the early 1950s, a truth partly obscured by Kerouac himself when he told Steve Allen in a TV interview that he wrote the book in three weeks.

There are readerly biases at play here—the first draft's allure of inspiration is also wedded to the allure of authenticity—which, since all writers begin as readers, we share. But writers also have a few anti-revision biases of our own.

All writers—even those, like me, with feet of clay—are seduced by the myth of the genius for whom it all comes quickly and easily, fully sprung from the head of Zeus, or dictated by the muse. Rare as that is, it's often the common formative experience of writing our very earliest stories. They come unbidden, surprising and delighting us, and they go unrevised. They represent something like a state of writing innocence, one to which we cling and yearn to return to (one reason why we keep writing). Revision by these lights might seem like a fallen art, a bit grubby when it's set alongside shining inspiration. Talent, genius—these are supposed to make things easier. Revision, on the other hand, looks like work, effort. That's both its appeal (for the humble) but also its stigma.

Dare I—as a Brit—even suggest there may be an *American* resistance to revision? Consider the tendency to see the Constitution as a perfect document, one to be read, in certain quarters at least, as if divinely inspired, holy writ. There's a familiar divide implied here between those who believe the Union to be perfect and those who seek to continue to perfect it, or in more threadbare terms, between the conservative and the progressive. Both sides, of course, are apt to accuse the other of being "revisionist." Still, it may be salutary, next time you're feeling resistant to revision, to consider that you're aligning yourself with strict originalists; all writers, however liberal, may have a streak of conservatism in that sense. As an antidote, it might help to recall that the framers were also revisers—of a nation, of government. It might even embolden us to think of revision as *revolution*, or at the very least as an effort to "form a more perfect" next draft. I have some reservations about "perfection" as a goal of revision, as I'll get to, but the apparent contradiction of "more perfect" seems a fitting aspiration for the tantalizing, ever-receding process of revision.

In short, we all—readers and writers alike—tend to associate inspiration with first drafts, and perspiration with what comes later, a cultural bias that informs the lingering distrust for writing programs, as well as the general scanting of revision.

Kerouac himself was probably both acceding to as well as perpetuating the myth, and before we accuse him of any self-aggrandizing burnishing of his own legend, we might reflect how for all writers—prone as we are to a squirming embarrassment, if not downright shame, at our fledging efforts—revision is in a sense an act of forgetting our earlier mortifying drafts, an act of forgetting moreover that manages to forget even itself. That's why the examples cited here feel like such rarities. Final drafts tend to erase those that come before them and a successful revision invariably covers its own tracks. Asked why he doesn't keep rough drafts, Tobias Wolff answers for most of us, I think: "They embarrass me, to tell you the truth" (albeit he also admits to enjoying reading the first drafts of others). Even those writers who do save them, perhaps with a view to selling them to an archive, tend to imagine them only being examined posthumously, though that too has its potential embarrassments. Wolff has suggested elsewhere that doubts about how much Gordon Lish influenced Raymond Carver's work might be another good reason to destroy drafts.

If the myth of the muse seems an ancient veil for revision, new technologies of writing—most obviously the displacement of the typewriter by the computer—have also contributed to its invisibility.

The aura of that Kerouac manuscript surely owes something to having been written on a typewriter, a now antique and increasingly totemic writing instrument (even *fetishized*, in the case of Kerouac's fellow Beat, William Burroughs, whose own grandfather was a manufacturer of them). Witness my novelist friends who collect them, or a pair of cuff links I own made from old keys, or the logo of my local bookstore.

I'm (just) old enough to have started writing on a typewriter—a member of the last generation of writers to precede the advent of the word processor. I got mine in high school but ended my undergraduate days in the late 1980s writing on a dedicated word processor (diskettes—check! dot-matrix printer—check!), around the same time as the first word-processed fiction—by Stephen King, Tom Clancy, or Frank Herbert, according to competing claims—was appearing in print. Thus I've a firsthand sense of both the painstaking work of revision on a typewriter (whether at the word or line level using Wite Out, or at the page or paragraph level requiring actual cutting and pasting, or simply the retyping of long stretches of text) and the seduction of that winking cursor with its promise of infinite easy revision.

The freedom to revise as much as one liked, the

electronic speed of those changes, and the flawless (typographically speaking) results were almost miraculous to typewriter users. It's no accident that the software of the day was called things like Word Perfect or Perfect Writer (likewise, the fact that my students now use a package called Scrivener betrays a nostalgic yearning for simpler writing technologies). Amy Tan, a trail-breaking early adopter, has noted another dimension of that freedom: how working on the computer released her from the anxiety of committing to paper and using up resources.

All this might suggest that the virtual nature of text on a screen encourages revision (though some studies have noted that writers who work on a computer tend to revise more at the level of word and sentence than at the level of content and structure). But there's also an argument that the word processor's ability to make a text look prematurely "finished"—thanks to font options and justified text—militates against revision, in a way that the relative imperfection of typescript does not. Our manuscripts essentially look publishable long before they are.

In my own experience I've certainly noticed a tendency, enabled by word processing, to focus revision on specific problem areas in a manuscript—this page, this scene, this chapter. That's a valuable way of focusing, of breaking down difficulties into manageable, localized issues, but also one that sometimes neglects the big picture, in a way that those old-school revisers who finished a typewritten draft and started over from the beginning likely did not. I sometimes call this the United Nations approach to revision—we parachute into the trouble spots, but sometimes at the risk of over-looking the global ramifications of our changes.

I don't mean to sound like a Luddite here. I'm writing this on a laptop, as I do all my work, and the literary world is already too prone to various forms of nostalgia (the next time a review compares a work to Dickens or Chekhov, ask yourself if you—or the critic—wouldn't rather be reading Dickens or Chekhov). Besides, questions about the technology of writing predate the word processor. Concerns about the sheer speed of composition allowed by the keyboard—whether the fingers might outstrip the brain—go back as far as the typewriter itself. Mark Twain claims to have been "the first person in the world to apply the type-machine to literature" (he submitted the first typewritten manuscript, for *Life on the Mississippi*, in 1882, although it was likely keyed by an assistant, also known as a typewriter in the parlance of the day). But Twain also complained to the Remington company that the machine corrupted his morals by making him want to swear (recalling his advice, "Substitute 'damn' every time you're inclined to write 'very'; your editor will delete it and the writing will be just as it should be").

Further back, Jane Austen used straight pins to attach patches to the text of her unfinished novel *The Watsons* (the holes are still visible on the manuscript). Earlier still, our very concept of a palimpsest ("a parchment or other writing-material written upon twice, the original writing having been erased or rubbed out to make place for the second") also derives from writing "technology" and its relation to revision. Early parchment, a valuable commodity, was washed with a mixture of milk and oat bran, to be reused, but over time the original underlying text would reappear. Come to think of it, the abiding fascination of the Kerouac manuscript may not be that it's typed, but that it's a *scroll*, a dated writing technology magically producing an ancient one.

"We shape our tools," as Marshall McLuhan has observed, "and thereafter they shape us."

The personal computer's subtle and radical reshaping of the revision process is likely another reason why writers sometimes struggle to understand revision. Consider the basic idea of the draft, the notion that revision is measured draft by draft, and the regular conversations that arise in interviews with writers about how many drafts a story or novel has gone through. Discussion of discreet drafts made sense in the era of the typewriter. An author might type their way through a draft, mark it up, and retype it, and repeat until done, each iteration yielding a new pile of pages, a distinct and easily numbered draft. But it makes a lot less sense to talk about a third draft or a thirtieth in an era of word processing, when a text is subject to almost continuous revision, infinite drafts, if you will, one saved on top of the other in the hard drive, numbered only when printed out to be shared with a workshop, or an editor, or an agent. Or even for bragging rights! As Colson Whitehead satirically advises: "Remove a comma and then print out another copy—that's another draft right there. Do this enough times and you can really get those numbers up, which will come in handy if someone challenges you to a draft-off." More soberly, Philip Roth noted of his early experiences with a computer: "I'm doing so much changing as I go along that the drafts disappear, as it were, into the rewrites." The concept of the draft, while it remains useful, has thus become more fluid and elusive.

The easy erasure of earlier words and lines that word processing allows further contributes to the invisibility of revision—it's quite possible now to envisage a finished story of which only one draft survives, all the earlier ones having been overwritten (the new academic specialization of digital forensics is devoted to recovering them)—and perhaps also to the nagging uncertainty about it. It's hard to measure progress, after all, if you can no longer see where you started from.

Even the language we use for these kinds of changes—tinkering, fiddling—suggests that ease may have somehow devalued the activity.

Interestingly, several contemporary writers persevere with the old methods, or some combination of writing "technologies": starting in longhand on legal pads, say, before typing up later revisions, thus preserving some demarcation of drafts. Anne Tyler, as she told the *New York Times*, subscribes to an even more elaborate process, perhaps in an effort to make the most of *all* available technologies: "She writes in longhand, draft after draft, and when she has a section she's satisfied with, types it into a computer. When she has a completed draft she prints it out and then rewrites it all in longhand again, and that version she reads out loud into a Dictaphone." Tyler would seem to be re-seeing (literally re-vising) and even re-hearing her work at various of these iterations, holding off that settled aura of inevitability that a draft accumulates after we've read it too many times in the same form.

The fresh sensory apprehension of an old draft is one reason I read my own work aloud and encourage my students to do the same (stressing that it's not enough to simply lip-sync it, however shy they might be about being overheard by roommates). Nicholson Baker, via his character Paul Chowder, even playfully advises doing so in different voices: "a juicy Dorchester accent, or a Beatles Liverpool accent, or a perfectly composed Isabella Rossellini accent."

Others try different strategies to defamiliarize and re-apprehend a draft: printing out pages and laying them out on the floor, say, for a kind of bird's-eye view of a narrative; reading sections or chapters out of order; boiling down a story to note cards or Post-its. Still others revise away from the desk, in their heads, while they're walking or, in my case, when I was starting out, while I was commuting on the T to shifts at a bookstore in Boston. Joan Didion goes so far as to advocate another kind of perceptual shift to loosen up for editing: "Really, I have found [a] drink actually helps" (a contrast to the older saw "write drunk, revise sober" attributed down the years to Auden, Dylan Thomas, Fitzgerald, Hemingway, and many more).

If technology complicates our understanding of revision, science in the form of a 2012 academic paper entitled "First Is Best" may clarify it. As its abstract states: "We experience the world serially rather than simultaneously. A century of research on human and nonhuman animals has suggested that the first experience in a series of two or more is cognitively privileged."

Coauthors Carney and Banaji dub this the "power of primacy" and go on to explain: "What is experienced first is remembered better, drives attachment more strongly, creates stronger association with the self, influences impressions more decisively, and persuades more effectively." It's not hard to see connections here to everything from nostalgia, to retro fashions, to first loves, to the clinging in old age to early childhood memories even as later ones fade. The researchers themselves hypothesize that the evolutionary roots of this automatic preference might lie in early attachment and the tendency for newborns to imprint on the first person they see, typically a parent.

To illustrate, in one of their experiments, subjects were asked to choose between two similar-looking sticks of bubble gum, and the researchers found that respondents picked the first they were shown (a statistically significant) 62 percent of the time, as opposed to the second, only 38 percent of the time. I'm partial to this particular example because gum is so humble, so down to earth. It's less easy to mythologize our preference because the first gum is more inspired or more authentic.

The real takeaway from this study, though, may be that those preference percentages—so heavily weighted in favor of the first choice—are only true when respondents are asked to make a *rapid* decision. When they were given more time for deliberation, they showed an equal preference for gum #1 and gum #2. The finding recalls one of my favorite pieces of writing advice: Flaubert's famous dictum that "Talent is long patience."

I confess when I first read that I suspected a bad translation from the French. But the older I get the more the call to patience resonates. I might even be tempted to rephrase Flaubert's line as "revision is long patience."

Or consider Dorothy Parker's famous—and widely shared—sentiment, "I hate writing; I love having written," as a corollary of which I might observe that we are, most of us, often indecently eager to finish whatever we're writing.

That haste makes intuitive sense in the case of first drafts. We're often racing our own skepticism—can I write this, is it worth anything?—in those early stages, praying to get to the end before our doubts overtake us. Building a bridge across a chasm of our own doubt. (Tellingly, Jane Smiley equates patience with faith.) There's an all or nothing feeling to first drafts. If we finish them we feel we have *something*, however flawed, to build on. As a friend says, "To make a silk purse, first get your sow's ear." But if we stop before the end, it's not clear we have anything at all. Is a bridge half finished even a bridge?

But what applies to first drafts needn't apply to later ones.

Rather, I might suggest, by way of paraphrase: Draft in haste, revise at leisure. Though strictly it's *not* a paraphrase, but a revision of the old adage "Marry in haste, repent at leisure" (attributed to Congreve in his play *The*

Old Bachelor, though it may owe a debt to Shakespeare's line from *The Taming of the Shrew*: "Who woo'd in haste and means to wed at leisure"). A first draft, by these lights, might be viewed as a kind of whirlwind romance, revision a mode of repentance!

The idea of revising at leisure, incidentally, points to one more subtle, but serious, impediment to revision. Leisure, patience, a new computer—these are all luxuries, after all. Writing in general is a privileged occupation, but some writers are luckier to be able to afford more time or technology than others. Revision, in that sense, is thus a gift, one granted or withheld by everything from individual circumstances to narrative form. As Neil Gaiman has noted: "I came from comics where I simply didn't have the liberty of rewriting a story until I was happy with it, because it needed to be out that month, so I needed to get it more or less right first time." It's easy to see how the same might be true for the writers of pulp fiction in the past (being paid by the word isn't likely to encourage revision), or even genre writers today, but it also applies to literary fiction. Consider Dickens writing for serialization, say. Or Hemingway and Fitzgerald, who, in the midst of producing lucrative stories for the then burgeoning commercial magazine market, saw their novels as labors of love (today the reverse might apply). More recently, I have older colleagues who came up in the 1960s and

1970s in a publishing environment where the expectation for literary writers was a new novel every couple of years (today five years or more seems typical), a regimen of productivity that allowed much less time to revise.

Finally, though, if we're apportioning blame here for the many misunderstandings of revision, we—teachers of writing, and the workshops we run—may have to take our share. Academic schedules, after all—the duration of a class, a semester, even a degree program—and the academic demands of deadlines and grades don't always align with the organic pace of revision, and certainly don't encourage patience.

More subtly, one common tenet of the writing workshop—one I subscribe to myself—is that we try to judge a story with respect to its author's intent. That's a respectful and pragmatic strategy in workshop. If a writer's goal is tragedy, then asking at the start of any discussion for more jokes seems to miss the point, dismiss the author, and likely means he or she won't listen to the suggestion (even if a case might be made that most tragedies could use a few more jokes, and that they might be all the *more* tragic for them). But this strategy—baked in as it is to many workshops—nonetheless bears examination. As I point out to my own classes, it rests on an assertion that we writers *know* our own intent in an early or first draft when I'd argue on the contrary that we rarely know ourselves or our work (which may amount to the same thing) so well at the outset.

I blame the common advice "write what you know" in general, and Hemingway in particular, for this idea of us "knowing" our stories. All those famous, bracing lines of his:

> I decided that I would write one story about each thing that I knew about.

> Write the truest sentence that you know.

Or—the so-called iceberg theorem:

> If a writer of prose knows enough of what he is writing about he may omit things that he knows and the reader, if the writer is writing truly enough, will have a feeling of those things as strongly as though the writer had stated them. The dignity of movement of an iceberg is due to only one-eighth of it being above water.

What comes out of these quotes is the *primacy* of knowing what we're writing about, the primacy of intent—*write what you* already *know*, is the implication—which in turn implies a kind of before-and-after model of writing. *Before*: we know what we want to write. *After*: we revise what we've written to better match *what we set out to write in the first place*. Revision by these lights becomes a process of perfection, the process of perfecting an initial platonic ideal of the story.

And there are a few problems with that.

In the first place, perfection can be an impossible, even dispiriting goal. If you've ever thought to yourself, despairingly, I could go on revising this *forever*, you've just taken a look down that ever-receding, infinitely regressing hall of mirrors that is perfection.

In the second place, the before-and-after/knowing-then-writing model again tends to imply that inspiration is restricted to the *before*, which makes the actual writing feel like about as much fun—which is to say as creative—as painting by numbers. We're back to "tidy your room."

In the third place, as you may have already realized, this just isn't how we do it, this isn't our actual experience of writing. What most of us already know is that writing is a mode of thinking; we think on the page (or as a friend once put it, "You can't spell THINK without INK"). As we write, as we express our initial thoughts, new ones spring to mind, to elaborate or complicate the initial ideas. We might call these inspirations, or more humbly surprises, but either way I suspect they're at the heart of the pleasure of the enterprise.

"Write what you know" does have value as advice. It speaks to the fundamental *author*ity of authorship, the contractual notion that if we ask for a reader's attention for thirty minutes or three hundred pages, we know something about our subject. But this speaks best to an end product, a final draft. The question we might ask is how we come to know what we know, and I suspect a guiding principle of early drafts might be better phrased as "Write *to* know," and of revision, "Revise to know more," and of a final draft, "I've written what I now know."

Other Hands, Other Eyes

By chance, my personal history—even before I became a writer—may have helped me part the mists obscuring revision. In my early teens, around the same time I was witnessing that act of bravery on my father's part, I was a science fiction fan. Hardly unusual, but my era of nerddom had some distinctive features. Back then movie release schedules were much different. While *Star Wars* was released in the US in May of 1977, fans in the UK had to wait until after Christmas before its release in British theaters, a seven-month delay that seems almost inconceivable now in our era of video piracy, streaming, and spoiler alerts. As an impatient eleven-year-old I was *desperate* for spoilers. I went in search of them in the form of newspaper articles and movie magazines and especially the novelization of the movie. Movie novelizations are something of a throwback today—now novels (and fan fiction) often extend the world of the movies and TV, back then they retold the movies and episodes themselves—but when I was a kid they were a staple of my reading (*Dr Who* novelizations, *Star Trek* novelizations), to be read and even reread, since before the advent of VCRs they were often the only way to relive a beloved movie. The words "soon to be a major motion picture" on a book cover were a siren song for me, potent as any blurb, so much so that even years later when I was offered the chance to write tie-ins for the *Kung Fu* TV series I was briefly tempted.

And the relevance of all this? Simply that the novelizations were often at variance with the movies, partly because (for scheduling reasons) they were based on treatments and early scripts rather than finished movies, partly because they were required to expand those hundred-page scripts into short novels. The novelizations thus contained scenes that never made the final cut (Luke Skywalker hanging out on Tatooine with friends, say) and language subsequently revised (the opening of the novelization of *Star Wars* refers to "Another galaxy, another time" rather than the now iconic "A long time ago in a galaxy far, far away"), as well as backstory and the internal reflections of main characters. All of these, to a child, were fascinating traces of revision. Even the *name* of the author wasn't above being changed: the novelization is credited to George Lucas rather than its ghostwriter, the prolific sci-fi author Alan Dean Foster (who also wrote, among others, the novelization for *Alien*—without ever being allowed to see a photo of the alien—and recently penned the tie-in to *The Force Awakens*). Looking back on this work, Foster noted that he took it for two reasons. First, because he was a young writer who needed to make a living. (He was reportedly paid a flat fee of five thousand dollars for a book that went on to sell more than three million copies in its first year.) And second, because "I got to make my own director's cut. I got to fix the science mistakes, I got to enlarge on the characters, if there was a scene I particularly liked, I got to do more of it, and I had an unlimited budget. So it was fun." This conclusion suggests some of the pleasures and rewards of revision. Lucas himself has gotten in on that fun, too, in the form of sequels, prequels, and special editions, even retitling that first movie *A New Hope*. (Titles, as we'll see later, are a rich but easily overlooked opportunity for revision.)

The upshot for me as a child was a sense of the flexibility of fiction, an appreciation for the myriad possibilities of change. Revision likely benefits from a nerdy obsession with detail, a geeky attention to nuance. Beyond this, the peek behind the curtain afforded by these revisionary traces made me conscious for the first time of the process behind a beloved movie— they were traces of *creativity*, essentially—which first sparked my own desire to create.

At a more exalted cultural level, I absorbed a similar lesson from the Shakespeare productions I started to see at the Royal Shakespeare Company in Stratford-upon-Avon—just a few miles from my home in Coventry—in my teens. A production of *Julius Caesar* featuring huge video screens relaying Anthony's speech at Caesar's funeral, or one of *The Merry Wives of Windsor* styled after P. G. Wodehouse, all plus fours and bowler hats, suggested the revisionary malleability of context.

Later, at college, taking my first degree in physics, I learned to massage—or "fudge"—my data to come up with the "right" results, a move reminiscent of the tinkering or fiddling often ascribed to revision, albeit with numbers rather than words. And later still, as I was finally attempting to reinvent myself as a writer in graduate school, a translation class impressed me with the sense of translation—the choice of this word, this emphasis, this meaning, or that—as quasi revision.

I have noted the invisibility and relative rarity of published revisions, as an antidote to which I've sometimes tried to offer my students—in the spirit of my own inadvertent apprenticeship—more mundane and familiar examples of what we might call "everyday" revision. Every movie adapted from a book (or vice versa in the case of novelizations), every cover version of a song, every sequel or remake or reboot of an old movie or TV show, every piece of fan fiction, offers forms of revision, albeit *revisions by another hand.* Understood in this light, revision is part of the postmodern air we breathe—"it surrounds us and penetrates us," just like the Force!—not so much invisible as hidden in plain sight. Our task is less to see it than to recognize it.

One more geeky example: His stint as governor of California notwithstanding, Arnold Schwarzenegger is best known for the role of the Terminator, whose iconic look—established in the second movie in the series—is biker leathers and dark glasses (itself a borrowing from earlier rebellious images like Marlon Brando's in the *The Wild One*). For those not familiar with these "classic" works, Arnold plays a time-traveling cyborg who arrives in our present from the future, naked (you can't send clothes through time, apparently, except via vintage stores), and thus needs at the start of several of the movies to acquire clothes, which he does in *Terminator 2* by beating up the denizens of a biker bar. In the third film, though, in a comic revision, he enters another seedy bar hosting . . . a bachelorette party, at which the entertainment is provided by a male stripper, who—you guessed it—is dressed in biker leathers (albeit more in the style of the Village People), which Arnold duly acquires.

The iconic image of Arnold in biker leathers—a timeless look for a time traveler—returns (he *did* promise "I'll be back") and yet its meaning has altered. It's now played for knowing, winking laughs, and we might even argue that a latent homoerotic meaning (think young, naked, body builder–buff Arnold) has been slyly surfaced.

A particular category of these revisions-by-another-hand is what is sometimes known as "the response story," a story or novel that repurposes an older narrative and speaks back to it. Jean Rhys's *Wide Sargasso Sea* with its response to *Jane Eyre* is a textbook example; Michael Cunningham's address to *Mrs. Dalloway* in *The Hours* (the original working title of Woolf's masterpiece) would be a more recent one. Famous stories have also gotten the treatment—there are multiple riffs on Chekhov's "Lady with Lapdog," for instance, by Joyce Carol Oates, Beth Lourdan, and David Means, among others (including a couple called, irresistibly, "The Lady with the Laptop").

Several works of this kind speak back politically to their predecessors, enacting a form of reverse cultural appropriation by the marginalized of the mainstream. Rhys's book is a postcolonial riposte to Brontë's, an early instance of what Salman Rushdie has described as "the Empire writes back." In similar vein, Derek Walcott's *Omeros* at once claims and repurposes Homer, whose *Odyssey* has also recently been reimagined from a feminist perspective by Margaret Atwood in her *Penelopiad*.

Other revisions of this ilk can be less ambitious, tilting toward playful homage (Helen Fielding's remix of Jane Austen for *Bridget Jones's Diary*) or leaning into parody (*Pride and Prejudice and Zombies*, anyone?). Still, it's possible to discern within some of them lessons for our own revision.

Hemingway's "The Killers" comes in for a fascinating and instructive example of this treatment in Ron Hansen's story, also called "The Killers" (first published in 1977, a full fifty years after its model).

In the original, Hemingway's young alter ego, Nick Adams, is a customer at a diner taken over by two hired guns who are lying in wait for a victim, a former boxer called Ole Andreson, but known as the Swede. They menace Nick and the staff at the diner, but leave when Andreson fails to show up for dinner, at which point Nick—in an act of bravery, and against the advice of the counterman at the diner—hurries to the Swede's boarding house to warn him. The climax—a purposeful anticlimax, in fact—is the Swede's impassive, fatalistic reception of this warning. He thanks Nick but declines to run or take any action to save himself. The story is thus a kind of coming-of-age moment in which young Nick runs up against existential resignation.

Hemingway is famed for having revised the last page of *A Farewell to Arms* thirty-nine times, but we don't have a lot of details about his revision process for "The Killers." An earlier draft seems to have been called "The Matadors" (boxers and bullfighters are recurring figures in Hemingway's work, of course). It's also thought that the story was inspired by the likely mob murder of a Chicago fighter called Andre Anderson in 1926. Finally, there's a 1916 piece of juvenilia—a comic anecdote that owes much to Ring Lardner—dating from

Hemingway's junior year at Oak Park High and published in the school's magazine, featuring a fixed fight and a character called "The Swede."

Hansen's version, which imagines the killers more fully as characters and follows their subsequent careers, is unabashed in revisiting the original scene, even down to lifting/quoting dialogue. But his version also offers this:

> Max watched the clock. At 7:10, when the Swede still hadn't shown, Max got off his stool. Al came out from the kitchen hiding the shotgun under his coat.
>
> "So long bright boy," Al said to the counterman. "You got a lot of luck."
>
> "That's the truth," Max said. "You ought to play the races."
>
> They went out the door and crossed the street.
>
> "That was sloppy," Al said.
>
> "What about where he lives?"
>
> "I don't know this town from apples."
>
> They sat down on the stoop of a white frame house. Inside a man and woman were leaning toward a crystal radio. There were doilies on their chairs and the man slapped his knee when he laughed. Part of a newspaper blew past Max's shoes. He snatched it and opened it up. Al nudged him when the kid in the leather jacket came out of Henry's. They followed the

kid up beside the car tracks, turned at the arc light
down a side street, and stood in the yard across from
Hirsch's rooming house. The kid pushed the bell and
a woman let him in.

The dialogue in the diner at the start of this section
is straight from Hemingway's original, but rather than
stay with Nick after the killers leave, Hansen choses
to follow *his* killers outside, where we see that Nick
(it's him in the leather jacket) in his subsequent act of
bravery and compassion in trying to warn the Swede
is, ironically, the very mechanism that leads the killers
to their victim. The story's events and their outcome
remain basically unchanged, but a new meaning, a
new *potential* in the narrative—missed or rejected by
Hemingway—has been unearthed to deepen and complicate the story.

"The Killers" is among Hemingway's most iconic
stories—its dialogue is also quoted in Tobias Wolff's
"Bullet in the Brain" whose doomed protagonist is
named Anders—and has also been subject to several
movie adaptations, notably a 1946 version starring Burt
Lancaster and Ava Gardner and a 1964 version with
Lee Marvin, Angie Dickinson, and Ronald Reagan (in
his final film role before a career revision of his own:
announcing his bid for governor of California the following year). In both film adaptations, the murderous

events of the short story serve as a dramatic prologue to an investigation of why Ole (still a boxer as played by Burt Lancaster, but a retired race driver, called Johnny North, as portrayed by John Cassavetes in the later version) became a target. In both cases the love of a femme fatale—Gardner and Dickinson, respectively—leads the unfortunate sporting hero into a life of crime. Hemingway's own elision of any backstory for Ole likely counts as an example of leaving out what you know. As he said himself of "The Killers": "That story probably had more left out of it than anything I ever wrote."

There are myriad variations between the original story and the two films, of course, but the later adaptation also serves as a revision of the earlier movie, maintaining its plot device of an investigation of Ole's backstory, for example, but retooling it.

In the earlier version, it's an insurance investigator, that staple of noir, who uncovers Ole's past (much of it shown in flashback); in the later movie, the investigation is now conducted by the killers themselves (they've been anonymously contracted for the hit and so don't know the "why" of it). In doing so they take on the narrative function of the insurance man while eliminating him as a figure, exhibiting the kind of streamlining and condensation that is often a hallmark of revision. But they *also* more subtly take on Nick's role from the original short story. There's a vestigial

Nick figure in the 1946 movie, but in the absence of an equivalent in the later film, Nick's existential disquiet— why does the Swede seem to welcome death?—is now granted to his killers, who are puzzled and unsettled by their victim's passivity. The conflation of Nick and the killers in this respect might even obliquely anticipate Hansen's intuition of Nick's ironic and unwitting complicity in the murder.

Around about this point in any conversation with my students about revision, someone in the room "gets it" and points out that there's another high-visibility form of revision familiar from pop culture: retroactive continuity, known increasingly by its abbreviated form, retcon.

Retcon can take various forms—to fill a plot hole from an earlier version of the narrative, or even to erase an element of that earlier version. Examples abound from the world of comic books, but staying, loosely, within the set of examples already to hand, the recent *Star Wars* spin-off *Rogue One* represents a retcon of the original movie in that it explains the otherwise rather too narratively convenient existence of the Death Star's fatal flaw (the weak point of the exhaust port that Luke torpedoes is in fact a flaw *designed* to sabotage the super weapon by a dissident scientist). A rather less well received example was George Lucas's decision to change the special edition of *Star Wars: A New Hope* to suggest that Han Solo killed Greedo only after being shot at first.

More bluntly still, the fifth Terminator film (*Terminator: Genisys*) ignored the events of the third and fourth films, as if they had not happened, only for its own disappointing box office results to ensure that it too was ignored by the next film in the series (*Terminator: Dark Fate*, for those keeping track). The ultimate instance, perhaps, of the forgetfulness of revision, although, given the centrality of time travel to the series and its characters' own struggles to achieve or resist retconning *within* the story, this seems only appropriate.

Retcon, as these examples suggest, tends to apply to long-running, serial works. An early literary example is the return of Sherlock Holmes, who, despite apparently dying at the Reichenbach Falls in "The Final Problem," was brought back a decade later by Conan Doyle in "The Empty House." A more egregious instance would be the infamous ninth season of the prime-time soap *Dallas*, which turned out to be "all a dream" in order to allow the resurrection of a character (Bobby Ewing, played by Patrick Duffy, who decided to return to the show). Retcon, as these examples imply, can be firsthand (Doyle) or secondhand (the respective scriptwriters of movie and TV series). What these instances share, and what's distinctive about retcon, is that it's typically (often risibly) visible to viewers and readers. It's revision-in-plain-sight in a sense, revision-on-the-fly, or—like J. K. Rowling's revelation that Dumbledore was gay—revision-post-publication (unlike most revision that we hope is prepublication).

In certain special circumstances, this visible revision can be an asset. The genre of alternate history, say, invites us to appreciate how the fiction we're reading revises reality. It's required that we know that Charles Lindbergh does *not* become president as we read Philip Roth's *Plot Against America*, or that the Axis *didn't* win the war in Philip K. Dick's *Man in the High Castle*, and indeed that Hillary *didn't* refuse Bill in Curtis Sittenfeld's *Rodham*.

These exceptions notwithstanding, the blatancy of retcons suggest a truth about revision, and a reason for its invisibility: revision seeks to be unseen, or at least to render what came before unseen. The invisibility of revision that we've been bemoaning is thus no accident, but rather a hallmark of *successful* revision. This most subtle skill of writers is the one that is not only least visible, but that actively aspires to invisibility.

That said, a vestige of retcon, of revision-on-the-wing, can often be glimpsed in novels—a form with deep, traditional roots in the serial. To take a trivial example, by way of illustration, imagine we criticize a

story for having a passive main character. Assuming
the writer considers the criticism valid, they may seek
to make their protagonist more active in subsequent
drafts. But now imagine the first chapter of a novel
that features a passive character. A writer taking that
feedback on board might choose not to revise chapter one, but alternatively to make the character more
active in chapter two or three, revising the book as it
moves forward (indeed, this kind of "revision" may be
indistinguishable from the kind of character or plot development that sustains a novel). This understanding
of novelistic revision might also go some way toward
resolving a recurrent dilemma that novelists face—
whether to revise mid-draft, or press on to the end of a
draft. There's no "right" answer to this for every writer,
or every project, but it might come as some relief to
consider that revision and pressing on aren't necessarily an either/or.

A more sophisticated illustration of the same principle might be the common tendency of novels to reorganize themselves—take a temporal or geographical leap,
switch characters, or make a structural departure—
midcourse. Consider a couple of notable recent works
by Susan Choi (*Trust Exercise*) and Lauren Groff (*Fates
and Furies*), both of which enact startling course-
correcting "revisions": in each case part two not only re-
tells but tellingly alters part one. Both novels essentially

shift point of view, a move that often creates drama and interest via a sense of competing and contrasting versions. More specifically, both Choi's and Groff's novels seem to radically reorganize themselves at the midway point, *as if* the writer has had second thoughts (though both shifts are deeply organic to the overall effects of the respective works). If Choi and Groff are consciously dramatizing revision—taking revision as their subject, in a sense—my own experience of this kind of course correction has been less intentional. That was certainly true in the writing of *The Welsh Girl* and my second novel, *The Fortunes*, both of which were significantly (and stressfully) reimagined on the fly. But what felt at the time like a crisis in the composition also feels in retrospect like a potential boon for those novels. After all, as much as any novel strives to create readerly expectations (which make us read on), it is also invested in subverting those expectations (which is what make a book unpredictable). That can be true of a character's trajectory, but equally of an established structure or style. This reorganization, or pattern-breaking, or subversion, call it what you will, might be understood as a result of a novel's dawning self-consciousness (often spurred on by some difficulty in the writing), of a novel beginning to read itself. To see itself, and then to re-see itself, in a revisionary process.

One further way of understanding this would be to

consider the "boot-strapping" problem that most novels present. Consider that if we write to know, then for
many novels, we need to write a first draft in order to
know, to learn, the story we're telling. This is part of the
thrill of a first draft, the excitement . . . and the anxiety,
because at the outset of this glimpsed, intuited, but in
crucial ways *unknown* story we're nonetheless obliged
to make certain decisions—structure, voice, style, tense,
point of view, and so on—about how best to tell it, essentially. We need to make those decisions to begin . . .
and yet those decisions can only be provisional until
we better know our own story, via the writing that follows. To put this knotty problem another way: we can
only decide how best to tell our story when we know it;
but we can only know it by first telling it. The result is
a feedback loop in which commonly we discover late or
even midway through a draft that the way we're telling
our story is limited (or limiting) in some way, that it isn't
the best way to tell the story we're uncovering—a discovery that obliges us to restart (hopefully in a better-
informed way) or to radically reorganize our story to go
on. This is why getting to the end of a first draft for a
novel is so hard, and so often a misnomer—the draft we
finish is rarely the one we embarked on.

These varied examples, many of secondhand revision,
hopefully go some way to demystifying revision and dis-

pelling its cloak of invisibility, what we might call the fog of inspiration. The most important point is the sheer ubiquity of revision, the sense that models of it are to be found almost everywhere we look, if only we know what to look for.

To see revision yet more clearly, to build on the hints here of what it is (and is not), and to begin to think of some ways to better go about it, I want to return to the firsthand experience of it from my prologue. How do we now see, or re-see, that episode?

We might recall that the first version, with my father, was drawn from life, the second, Rotheram's, a fictional reimagination. In that sense even the earliest draft of the passage in the novel was *already* a revision. Indeed, anything we write that draws from life—our own, a newspaper story (where Hemingway likely first learned of Andre Anderson's fate), historical research—is always and already a revision (and in all but the first of these instances also revision-by-another-hand). Anything recollected is inevitably a revision of the original experience, an amalgam of the recalled, the forgotten, and the imagined. As Kate Walbert notes: "Memory is just another draft of a story." By these lights, the version of the true events I recounted at the start, and presented as the original, is itself a revision of those events, and one written for *this* book, which is to say later than the passage from the novel that purportedly revises it.

And (temporal paradox aside!) this should actually be heartening. To the plaintive question how do we revise, we can now answer: We already do, we already are, we can't help it. Recognizing that even our first drafts have antecedents dissolves the artificial division—the line in the sand we sometimes hesitate to cross—between creation and revision, and serves as a corrective to our first-is-best bias.

I'd go so far as to say all writing is revision, and all writers are revisers at heart. Hemingway approaches this in his famous axiom, echoed by many others, that "the only kind of writing is rewriting," but Walbert's statement suggests that revision may even precede writing, that it's a fundamental attribute of imagination.

Consider, if you will, what I've sometimes described as the Ur-moment for all writers, when someone in the schoolyard cracks wise at our expense. We've all experienced that, and the concomitant moment of tongue-tiedness, when we were denied the snappy comeback, the witty riposte. Those moments befall us all, but writers, I suspect, are apt to dwell on such moments, revisit them, and typically—a few minutes, or hours, or days, or, if we're really obsessed, years later—come up with the line we should have delivered (the French have an elegant term for this: *l'esprit d'escalier*, literally "staircase wit"). That is, we *revise* the past. And this, I'd argue, is the germ of what makes us want to be writers, to revise life, often for the better (to make ourselves the heroes and not the butts of such moments), in wish-fulfillment fashion, albeit sometimes, in more sophisticated work, for the worse, to explore a kind of fear fulfillment. It's no accident that the characters in my own work—but also in that of many writers—are driven by regret, by guilt, and by shame.

Which brings me back to my initial example.

I began with the question of what changed between that Coventry street scene and the one in Berlin, and while we might point to period, context, action, and characters, I'd go further and—following the example of Hansen's retelling of Hemingway—suggest that the sum of these changes is that the *meaning* of the episode has been altered.

Oh, we could argue that both versions of my story share a political meaning. Both versions broadly indict racist violence—an indictment magnified by the echo across time (the skinheads are neo-Nazis). But I'd contend that the meaning of the episode, at the *character* level, has been significantly modified. One instance is an example of courage—my father's—with all the hope that brings. The other, with its focus on the passive, paralyzed witness, is an instance of something else: not cowardice per se, but perhaps the *fear* of cowardice—my own. Let's call it guilt: bystander guilt, survivor guilt. Something unresolved that readers anticipate might play out in the narrative to come.

I mentioned earlier that my father—the hero—isn't

in the revision, but that's not quite true. He *is* present in some ghostly, refracted form, in the figure of Rotheram's mother and her warning "not to get involved" in such attacks, which is what my father told me after the incident I witnessed. Think of that. Here was a moment of heroism on the part of my father, a moment when I was most proud of him, and yet his reaction was to warn me off such acts of bravery, to tell me essentially *not* to be like him at precisely the moment when I most wanted to be. That's a protective parental instinct, of course—I was twelve—but one I interpreted as a child as a lack of faith in me, a sense that if I was called on in a crisis I would be found wanting. I couldn't begin to articulate that at the time, but as an adult, writing about it, and via an older character's point of view in Rotheram, I was able to make it an essential narrative conflict.

I talked earlier about the meaning of the episode being altered, but it might be fairer to suggest that this other meaning was already inherent in the event. Revision hasn't changed it so much as uncovered it, brought it forward into the light. In doing so the emphasis of the episode has shifted; the stress is no longer on bravery, but on cowardice.

The point to reiterate here is that for all the changes to setting and character, for all the basic, recognizable terms that remain, what's changed, or deepened, is what the episode means, how it feels. *That's* what revision adds up to.

I should note that there's arguably yet a third revision of these events in my 2016 novel, *The Fortunes*, shifted this time to Detroit in 1982 and superimposed on a real-life hate crime: the murder of Vincent Chin, a Chinese American mistaken for a Japanese by two autoworkers resentful about the competition from foreign car imports.

> It was Vincent's idea. He told me to run. Only he didn't say *run*. He said, "Scram." It was the last word I heard from him in English, so I've given it a lot of thought. *Scram.* It's what you say to a kid, isn't it? A nuisance. Or maybe what naughty kids say to each other after they ring a doorbell. Scram. Not run. *He* was a runner. Running to him meant winning. Running *toward* something. Scram, I think, meant running away. If he'd said *run* we might both have run, but *scram* was for me. Because he didn't scram. He waited for them. He could have gotten away. When Evans hopped out of the car—a Plymouth, for the record—it was still moving. It ran over his foot, for god's sake! It was the Keystone Klan out there! You think Vincent couldn't have outrun these guys? He lettered in track. But he was done running. He

started it at the club, after all. He would have fought in the gravel and dog-shit parking lot outside too if Evans hadn't gone for the bat. He *wanted* to fight them. Maybe he figured he could make Evans drop the bat, shame him into a fair fight. Maybe he figured just two on one they wouldn't feel they needed the bat.

This was on Woodward, under the golden arches there, fluorescent tubes in the sign humming like cicadas.

I didn't run far. To the edge of the light. Just far enough to live, just far enough to watch.

Scram! Who was he to tell me to scram? Who was I to listen?

He was grappling with Pitts when Evans caught him across the knees, as if reaching for a grounder, after which Vincent couldn't have run even if he'd wanted. Then a line drive to the chest—*pop!*—as he went down, two more to the head when he was on all fours. Swinging for the fences.

I ran back, but too late. Before or after the two off-duty cops working security at the Mickey D's drew on Evans? You might wonder. Me too.

Vincent's last words—"It's not fair"—to me, in Chinese, while I cradled his ruined head, blood bubbling from his mouth and nose as he spoke, blood pouring from his ears like oil. His skull felt like rotten

fruit. I thought I'd pissed myself, but the warm wetness
in my lap was his brains.

I describe this as "arguably" another revision because unlike the version in *The Welsh Girl* I wasn't consciously recapitulating that Saturday with my father
when I wrote this scene (I was naturally more focused
on retelling the circumstances of Chin's death). And
yet the echoes—which only came to me as I worked on
this book—seem inescapable in retrospect (revision revealed again as an act of forgetting).

The setting has altered once more, as have the events,
but several important elements doggedly persist, albeit
in starkly intensified form, most obviously the point of
view of a witness/survivor whose guilt is now magnified threefold—he flees, the victim is a close friend,
the assault is more brutal and ends more tragically. In
other subtle ways this version is actually closer to the
original than the retelling in *The Welsh Girl*. Detroit
in 1982 bears striking similarities to Coventry in 1979.
They were both cities founded on their auto industries
and both at this time subject to economic decline and
a rise in racial animus driven by economic anxiety (a
couple of years later the Coventry band the Specials
would capture the mood to grim perfection in their
hit "Ghost Town"). That's likely why, even as a teenager
in Britain, the Vincent Chin story resonated with me

when I first heard it. The target of the racism in this version is also closer to home—closer to the original, closer to me. Even the trope of running, of a foot race, has its analog, although this time it's the victim who stands his ground, the witness who runs, at once an inversion and a conflation.

Speaking of fathers and sons . . . decently well read literary critics might have already recognized, especially in my discussion of Hemingway and Hansen, some similarity to the seminal arguments of Harold Bloom on the "anxiety of influence." Bloom's phrase, coined in his 1973 book of the same name, posits a quasi-oedipal relationship between living writers and the dead, the living obliged to wrestle with the influence of the past. In crude terms, those who've come before us are fathers, or parents, that we must rebel against and reckon with. We are inspired to write by these past models—all writers begin as readers—but live in fear of never escaping or transcending their influence, of remaining in their thrall forever (of essentially writing nothing but fan fiction). Bloom's is a far-ranging thesis—at once subtle and erudite—and one I wouldn't dare to try to do justice to here, let alone to the debates it has provoked. But I do want to look briefly at the mechanism he describes by which the living wrestle with the dead, essentially speaking back to their precursors. He describes these as "revisionary ratios"—a provocative term in our current context—and lists six of them by which young writers (Bloom focuses on poets) grapple with those who've come before.

Two of his ratios—which he calls *clinamen* and *tessera*—resonate especially with me. The first is defined as "a corrective movement . . . which implies that the precursor poem went accurately up to a certain point, but then should have swerved, precisely in the direction that the new poem moves." The second describes a process whereby a younger poet "'completes' his precursor, by so reading the parent-poem as to retain its terms but to mean them in another sense, as though the precursor had failed to go far enough."

These are dense, involved definitions, but ones that should recall some of the works we've already spoken of.

In the most trivial case, the outfit of biker leathers that Arnold Schwarzenegger's character obtains in *Terminator* 2 and 3 might be seen as "retained terms" that in the second version "mean in another sense" (comic and/or homoerotic).

In a more sophisticated instance like Hansen's retelling of Hemingway, we might suggest that the "swerve" is the recognition that Nick leads the killers to their target, a dark irony that the original didn't go far enough in pursuing. Hansen's version is explicitly a narrative of oedipal influence: a younger killer ends up stalking one of Hemingway's original, now aged hitmen, who in his later years not only resembles a bearded Hemingway but ends up committing suicide by shotgun. (Hansen's story, indeed, might owe as much to Bloom as to Hemingway.)

What I'd further suggest—a suggestion that goes beyond Bloom (or *swerves* from him, perhaps)—is that these revisionary ratios apply not only between writers and their precursors, but also between drafts *by the same writer*. By these lights, early drafts are among *our* precursors, parents of the next draft, and our task is to read them, closely and critically, to see where we might "swerve" from them, where we might retain their terms but mean them differently, and how we might take them further. Work that the iterations of that story about my father and me on that Coventry street are engaged in.

Remakes, reboots, retcons, sequels, revisionary ratios . . . all of these ideas, I hope, are helping to draw revision out, and to suggest that it's not at heart "only" an issue of craft—which tense to choose, which point of view, whether to change the period or setting or action—but rather what these choices amount to, what they serve, which is the elaboration, articulation, alteration, and enriching of meaning.

A vision of revision, if you will, begins to emerge, of

revision as an *ongoing* process of creativity, inspiration, and discovery, in which we continue to learn, to refine our intent, to come to understand what our own stories mean as we *know* them better.

That work of understanding, of knowing, is familiar to all of us. We call it reading. And judging from most workshops I've taught, writers are generally very good at it, just as Ron Hansen is a very good reader of Ernest Hemingway.

If revision is invisible—deliberately in its technique as well as unconsciously as an act of forgetting or overwriting—it would seem that the best way to make it visible is via close and careful reading. That's something most writers practice on the work of others, but that revision asks us to practice upon ourselves and our own earlier drafts. To re-see, to revise, we need first to re-read.

And if revision is re-vision, re-seeing, we might understand it specifically as a shift from seeing our work through the eyes of its writer to seeing our work through the eyes of a reader. The first of those people— the writer—thinks he or she knows what they're doing, what they intend; the second, the reader, is trying to figure it out. The first mindset serves the first draft, the second serves revision.

As George Saunders puts it: "I try to base my revision on a re-reading of what I've done so far, imitating, so far as it's possible, a first-time reader. That is, I try not to bring too many ideas about what the story is doing etc, etc. Just SEE what it's doing."

But how do we enter that second mindset? How do we effect what amounts to a kind of gestalt shift and begin to see our work through the eyes of readers? There are a few ways.

If you're like me, you might work on a story until you despair of it—it's the worst!—stick it in a drawer, or bury it in a file on the computer. Neil Gaiman again: "If I can, I'll put it away for a week or two. Not look at it. Try to forget about it. Then take it out and read it as if I've never seen it before and had nothing to do with its creation." For me it takes a little longer—say, six months—until whatever I'm working on *currently* seems even worse, and that old piece not quite so bad. I dig it out, take a look, and somewhere in the intervening months—if I'm lucky—I might find I've forgotten why I made a particular choice, or what I thought an image meant. Forgetting, by these lights, is not only a goal of successful revision, but also a step toward it. Specifically, I'll have forgotten my half-baked, half-formed writerly intent and be obliged to *read* the story and rather than thinking I already *know* what it means, I'll have to *figure out* what it means. If we must think of intent, then, it may help to think less of *our* intent . . .

and think instead of the characters' intent, or the material's intent, or even the language's intent.

If six months seems a long time to wait between drafts—and it's not, ask Flaubert—here's some hope. Sharing work with readers—an editor, a workshop—is a great accelerant of this process. Hearing any reader's feedback, we start to see, we're sometimes rather uncomfortably *forced* to see, the story through their eyes. And typically, that happens even before they open their mouths. Think back to the moment in workshop when you hand out a piece, or the moment if you send out work to journals or competitions that you hit Send or drop the envelope in the mailbox. Those are moments of trepidation, followed a second later by a typical realization: "Shit, I meant to fix *that*!" Except it's not forgetting something we meant to do. It's not looking back—it's looking forward, remembering what we *will* do. And it happens because you are already anticipating other eyes on the piece, are already beginning to see it with a reader's perspective. Revision by another hand turns out to be just a subset of revision through other eyes.

Suck It and See

We've arrived at the middle of our story of revision, and as all writers know, middles are hell. Dante gets it: "Midway on our life's journey, I found myself / In dark woods, the right road lost" (and those are just his opening lines!)

Or, to put it more prosaically, as several wags have noted: Every story has a beginning, a *muddle*, and an end.

Small wonder then that revision—the middle of the writing process; the journey from first to final draft—can feel like such a muddle at times, our own dark woods. But what if the "road lost" wasn't "right" at all? What if it were just the path we thought we knew, the way we intended to go, the one we assumed would be quickest when we set out? What if the journey instead were an exploration? Its destination to be discovered? Dante's lines, in that respect, offer a glimmer of hope—a light at the end of the tunnel—that even as we lose our path, we may yet find ourselves.

Perhaps instead of speaking of intentions, or what we know, it may help to modify our terms and to consider our initial sense of a story as a *hypothesis*, and what we know about it as provisional—*theory*, in essence. It follows that a draft might be seen as an experiment designed to test that hypothesis. This is science's mode of exploration and discovery, of course. And something I learned from my training as a physicist and my study of the history and philosophy of science: you need a hypothesis to design an experiment, but the experiment doesn't/shouldn't assume that the hypothesis is correct.

If the language of science sits uneasily in this discussion of fiction, remember that every story begins with a hypothetical: *What if?* Fiction indeed might be understood as a kind of thought experiment. What is a lie in search of the truth, after all—Picasso's definition of art—if not a form of provisional knowledge? (The very book you're reading partakes of the idea. Montaigne coined the term *essay* from the French *essayer* meaning "to try" or "to attempt," reflecting his original conception of his new form as a *test*.)

One typical, early hypothesis, common to many of us, is hinted at by that perennial question asked of authors, "Do you know the ending when you begin?" There are various answers to that question depending on which writer you ask, but an honest one for many might be "I *think* I know the ending," which is to say we have a hypothesis for how a story might end, a hypothesis moreover that in the writing, or afterward as we reread or hear feedback, we might discover to be wrong and seek to modify. We might find, say, that the story ends later than we thought. This is actually a pretty common revelation—the ends that we have in mind for first drafts are often climaxes, just as on any uphill route we only have eyes for the summit. But stories often continue on the other side, beyond their climaxes, into a denouement, or resolutions phase, the so-called falling action of Freytag's famous triangle (a limited model, but one that's useful for reminding us that climax and ending are distinct).

Other stories, we may discover, end sooner than we thought (*The Welsh Girl* at one point was supposed to reach all the way from World War II to the 1980s; its action is now confined to the mid 1940s). Still others may veer off along the way. A story of mine called "The Hull Case," about an interracial couple's UFO experience in the 1960s (based on a real couple, Betty and Barney Hill, and a real event, if one believes in such things) was originally intended to close with a viewing of the famous 1968 *Star Trek* episode "Plato's Stepchildren," in which Kirk and Uhura share one of the first interracial kisses on TV. As might be clear by now, that intersection with pop culture appealed to my inner nerd, but felt in the end like a too on-the-nose coda to the story.

While this notion of intent as a hypothesis to be tested serves as a useful concept for a first draft—it downgrades intent from something known or inspired to something less rigid like a "hunch" or a "lead"—it also applies as we move further into the revision process. New hypotheses can be tested *with each draft*—what if I cut this? what if I expand that? what if I shift the time frame? or the point of view?

Sometimes these are even the hypotheses of *others*—trusted readers, editors, and teachers. Personally, as a corrective to the danger of feedback devolving into a litany of what doesn't work, what needs to be cut, I try not only to focus on the difficulties in a draft, but also to suggest remedies and opportunities in a story that point the way toward additions as well as subtractions. There's a school of thought—well-meaning and respectful—that criticism shouldn't be prescriptive, often couched in sentiments like "It's your story and you should do whatever you want with it." But it feels to me that there's also something mildly disingenuous, even ungenerous, in a stance that says "Here are all the problems in your story . . . good luck!"

I once heard a coda to that famous saw that "imitation is the sincerest form of flattery": innovation is the sincerest form of criticism. It's in that spirit—the essence of *constructive* criticism—that I endeavor to offer solutions to the problems I identify in a story and encourage students to do the same for each other. We won't necessarily hit on the right answer, but the effort to offer one often sheds further light on the problem. In all likelihood, even if I and several others in a class identify a similar problem, we won't all offer the same solution, but that's for the good. It's hard for a class to be prescriptive if it can't agree on a single prescription, but it's nonetheless useful, and hopeful, for a writer to be offered several possible paths—or hypotheses—to choose from. Even if the suggestions originate elsewhere, those choices remain the writer's.

The challenge of moving forward with revision after a workshop's feedback is the overwhelming sense that there's simply so much to fix, so many choices, that we don't know where to even begin. An answer to that—after the model of a controlled experiment—might be to remind ourselves not to try to fix everything in one go, in one draft (there's that note of impatience again). Better perhaps to try to address a particular issue in a particular draft.

One specific instance of this difficulty occurs when adding new material to a story. In that case the first challenge is to generate the new material itself—let's say a new flashback. But a secondary challenge is to fit the new material into the existing draft—how and where might the flashback be introduced? If it runs long might it distract from or even swamp the present action? Problems tend to arise when we conflate the first challenge with the second. The new material may need to be long, but we instinctively curtail it because we're not sure how to squeeze it into the existing framework of the story. We're trying to solve two problems at once, and that divided focus can undermine our best efforts. I tend to work, and advise others to work, on new material on a fresh page, or in a new document. That allows me to focus on the new scene before worrying about how to incorporate it. What often happens in practice is that the new scene may run to a couple of pages of free writing before I find the crucial exchange, the paragraph or half page within it that I need to reinsert in the story. But if I don't allow myself the space to write long, I might never find the lines I need.

Even addressing one issue at a time is by no means easy, and indeed we often still balk at addressing the hardest revisionary questions, the ones where a possible solution isn't clear. This understandable hesitancy is a common reason we postpone or avoid revision altogether. As a first step, I often suggest *not* addressing the hardest issue first. Why not start with the easiest thing to fix—again our morale is supported—or better yet the one that seems most exciting or even fun? If you have the sense of "I know how to fix that" or "What I'd really like to add to the story is . . . ," those seem like excellent instincts to attend to (the latter especially the kind that leads to new discoveries in a draft). They make embarking on revision, the price of entry to the next draft, seem much less forbidding, something we do for ourselves and not as a chore assigned (any revisionary resistance is inevitably increased by a sense that we're being made to do it).

These are all strategies to make choice less daunting, but it remains inevitable, of course. The feedback of others, and our own critical intelligence, always present revisionary choices: call them, for the sake of simplicity, Door Number One and Door Number Two (though the hallway can have many more doors). Some people suggest one, some the other. Even if we agree with the diagnosis of a problem in a story, we may find ourselves paralyzed by the choice between revisionary responses. How to choose? Which is right? That paralysis tends to result in no choice being made.

But this, too, is a manifestation of impatience. We fear the wrong choice, because it will waste time, take us further from our finished, perfect story. So out of fear of making the wrong choice, we make no choice. But what's the worst that can happen? You make a choice, pursue it, discover it was wrong, and . . . go back to the previous draft. Is this wasted time, wasted endeavor? I'd rather call it a successful experiment. Door Number One is just another hypothesis to test via experiment. If you learn that Door Number One was a dead end, you may have also learned that Door Number Two is the right path.

The main thing is not to get hung up on the choice; try one and find out. The choice is hard because we have imperfect information. We can't foresee all the ways that a choice will play out. But the only way to rectify that, to get more information on which to make a sound choice, is to open a door and see where it leads. The only way to choose, in other words, is to choose. And sometimes the only way to choose the right option is to choose the wrong one first. (My shorthand for this piece of advice is "Suck it and see"—a Britishism referring to trying out something untested or unknown. Choice seems less daunting when it's imagined as a bowl of boiled sweets!)

What's essential to note here, a valuable part of the mindset of revision where maintaining morale is key to patience, is that an experiment *isn't* a failure if it disproves a hypothesis. For a scientist that's a success; it means something has been learned, that we now *know* more than we did before. If Thomas Kuhn's *Structure of Scientific Revolutions* is to be believed, experiments that don't conform to an expected theory are essential to progress, to the reinvention of theory, or as we might put it, the revision of science.

We're used to talking about experimental writers,

avant-garde artists who push the boundaries of form or style or language—readers can occasionally feel like *they're* the guinea pigs for such work—but in this sense all writers are experimenters.

This "experimental" mindset is nicely illustrated by the midcentury Irish writer Frank O'Connor, albeit that O'Connor himself might seem like the least experimental of writers. He's perhaps best remembered now for a handful of anthologized stories, notably "First Confession" and "Guests of the Nation" (itself the subject of a radical revision by another hand, this 1931 story of British prisoners in the hands of the IRA was an inspiration for Neil Jordan's film *The Crying Game*), but he published almost fifty stories in the *New Yorker*, and in 1961 when he taught a guest workshop at Stanford likely seemed both a very established and a very conventional writer to a class of young Turks that included Robert Stone, Larry McMurtry, and Ken Kesey. The workshop reportedly didn't go well (O'Connor suffered a stroke!), though his lectures on the short story were better received and later collected in his influential, if scattershot, book on the genre, *The Lonely Voice*. Sean O'Faolain memorably compared O'Connor as a critic to "a man who takes a machine gun to a shooting gallery. Everybody falls flat on his face, the proprietor at once takes to the hills, and when it is all over, and you cautiously peep up, you find that he has wrecked the place but got three perfect bull's-eyes."

O'Connor's approach to his own writing (and that of his students), outlined in a 1959 BBC broadcast called "Writing a Story—One Man's Way," can seem programmatic. "Before I start the serious business of writing a story I like to sketch it out in a rough sort of way," he says. "In class I insist on this blocking out of the story, which I call a treatment. The students all hate it." I bet! Specifically, O'Connor—sounding a bit like a forerunner of a screenwriting coach—advises writing out a story in advance in just four lines, a prescription he softens ever so slightly: "Four is only an ideal, of course; I don't really quarrel with five and sometimes a difficult subject may require six." As an example, he offers the skeletally schematic "X marries Y abroad. After Y's death, X returns home to Y's parents, but does not tell them Y is dead." Rigid as this process seems, O'Connor makes a case for its flexibility. Stripping a story of its specificity (setting, period, character, etc.), he contends, "gives me freedom— freedom to try out the story in terms of any place or group of people who happen to interest me at the moment."

While he probably wouldn't use the language, what this sounds like to me is a hypothesis (or maybe, to borrow another scientific term, an abstract) to put to the test in an experiment, in this case a draft. And indeed, O'Connor turns out to be a writer who not only revised his stories extensively over time, but even published various versions of them in subsequent volumes. As he puts it:

Those of you who know something about my work will realize that even then, when you have taken every precaution against wasting your time, when everything is organized, and, according to the rules, there is nothing left for you but [to] produce a perfect story, you often produce nothing of the kind. My own evidence for that comes from a story I once wrote called "First Confession." It is a story about a little boy who goes to confession for the first time and confesses that he had planned to kill his grandmother. I wrote the story twenty-five years ago, and it was published and I was paid for it. I should have been happy, but I was not. No sooner did I begin to re-read the story than I knew I had missed the point. It was too spread out in time.

Many years later a selection of my stories was being published, and I re-wrote the story, concentrating it into an hour. This again was published, and became so popular that I made more money out of it than I'd ever made out of a story before. You'd think that at least would have satisfied me. It didn't.

Years later, I took that story and re-wrote it in the first person because I realized it was one of those stories where it was more important to say "I planned to kill my grandmother" than to say "Jackie planned to kill his grandmother." And since then, you'll be glad to know, whenever I wake up at four in the morning and think of my sins, I do not any longer think of the crime I committed against Jackie in describing his first confession. The story is as finished as it is ever going to be, and, to end on a note of confidence, I would wish you to believe that if you work hard at a story over a period of twenty-five or thirty years, there is a reasonable chance that at last you will get it right.

Somewhere in these revisions he describes it's worth noting that the temporal point of view also changes. The first person he adopts in the final draft is a retrospective one, a temporal distance that crystalizes the darkly comic tone of "I planned to kill my grandmother." One might speculate that O'Connor's extreme example of patience—a revision decades in the making—may well have been integral to this key shift in temporal distance.

This wry narrative of revision, less the story of a story than the yarn of one in O'Connor's folksy voice, might seem contrary to his avowed idea of working the story out in advance, or to at least suggest the futility of the practice. But I suspect that the effort to outline is a response on his part to the protean nature of his (and all our) stories. Without a flawed hypothesis, we can't find our way to a true one.

Sore Thumbs

Despite such pithy observations as Capote's "I believe more in the scissors than I do in the pencil" or Nabokov's "My pencils outlast their erasers," the process I've begun to describe, as much additive as subtractive, suggests that revision isn't (only) editing, in the narrow sense of cutting or contraction. There's a time for erasers and scissors (and the Delete key), to be sure, but it's often later in the process than we imagine, or out of impatience allow for. Many second, and later, drafts need to expand rather than, or at least before, they contract. Early revisions, contrary to that "tidy your room" vibe, often become messier, necessarily so in order for us to explore and make discoveries.

Hemingway's line about leaving out, or cutting, what you know, returns here. But if most of us know *by writing*, then cutting too soon runs the risk that we may not have yet learned what we need to know about a story. Writing more expansively is thus likely to yield more knowledge. This is especially true when early drafts are written to deadline—for classes, or competitions or applications—and therefore often artificially constrained and abbreviated.

This expansion can take different forms. The common

advice to "write through" an ending might apply here, as might expansions of a secondary character's role, or the backstory of a major figure. There are opportunities to address pacing, which is often headlong in our early drafts, and never more so than in the final pages, where we tend to dip for the tape like runners in a sprint. A story isn't a race, and if we behave as if it is, we often end up leaving the reader behind. We may also intensify drama, as a tendency of early drafts—a natural one since we tend to sympathize with and identify with our creations—is to go easy on our main characters. Finally, we're apt in early drafts to glide over things that seem clear to us, already known, but that may be worth elaboration or clarification for readers.

Joyce's story "The Sisters," the first piece in *Dubliners*, offers a simple but instructive illustration of some of the possibilities of revisionary expansion.

It's the story of a boy learning of the death of an old priest who has taken him under his wing. In the earliest version—Joyce's first published story credited to Stephen Daedalus and appearing in the *Irish Homestead* in 1904—the youngster recalls the old man as follows:

> I often saw him sitting at the fire in the close dark room behind the shop, nearly smothered in his great coat. He seemed to have almost stupefied himself

with heat, and the gesture of his large trembling hand
to his nostrils had grown automatic. My aunt, who is
what they call good-hearted, never went into the shop
without bringing him some High Toast, and he used
to take the packet of snuff from her hands, gravely
inclining his head for sign of thanks. He used to sit in
that stuffy room for the greater part of the day from
early morning, while Nannie (who is almost stone
deaf) read out the newspaper to him. His other sister,
Eliza, used to mind the shop. These two old women
used to look after him, feed him, and clothe him. The
clothing was not difficult, for his ancient, priestly
clothes were quite green with age, and his dogskin
slippers were everlasting. When he was tired of hearing the news he used to rattle his snuff-box on the arm
of his chair to avoid shouting at her, and then he used
to make believe to read his Prayer Book. Make believe,
because, when Eliza brought him a cup of soup from
the kitchen, she had always to waken him.

It's a detailed, vivid evocation, but Joyce evidently
wasn't quite satisfied with it because when *Dubliners*
appeared ten years later the passage had been revised
as follows:

Had he not been dead I would have gone into the
little dark room behind the shop to find him sitting

in his arm-chair by the fire, nearly smothered in his great-coat. Perhaps my aunt would have given me a packet of High Toast for him and this present would have roused him from his stupefied doze. It was always I who emptied the packet into his black snuff-box for his hands trembled too much to allow him to do this without spilling half the snuff about the floor. Even as he raised his large trembling hand to his nose little clouds of smoke dribbled through his fingers over the front of his coat. It may have been these constant showers of snuff which gave his ancient priestly garments their green faded look for the red handkerchief, blackened, as it always was, with the snuff-stains of a week, with which he tried to brush away the fallen grains, was quite inefficacious.

Again we might ask, what's changed and why? The details are even more vivid, better *seen*—the little clouds of snuff smoke *dribbling* through the old man's fingers especially so—but there's also a greater organization and flow to the paragraph. Crucially, the detail of the snuff is now causally related to the "green faded" look of the priest's cassock. It's as if the older Joyce rereading the earlier draft had recognized that the two details—sharp, but unconnected—were more intimately woven together than first glimpsed or acknowledged, a recognition enabled perhaps by letting his point-of-view character more actively occupy the room. The earlier draft attends more to the sisters' ministrations to their brother; now, "It was always I who emptied the packet into his black snuff-box . . ." The effect is a sharpened image, as if a camera lens had been twisted into focus.

An instance of patience in revision is apparent at the end of the story. While patience gives us writers time to understand a story—to continue the photographic metaphor, gives time for the image of the story to develop—it can also manifest on the page to great effect for the reader. Consider the ending of the original draft, wherein we learn the secret of why the old priest is a little "off":

"It was that chalice he broke. . . . Of course, it was all right. I mean it contained nothing. But still . . . They say it was the boy's fault. But poor James was so nervous, God be merciful to him."

"Yes, Miss Flynn, I heard that . . . about the chalice . . . He . . . his mind was a bit affected by that."

"He began to mope by himself, talking to no one, and wandering about. Often he couldn't be found. One night he was wanted, and they looked high up and low down and couldn't find him. Then the clerk suggested the chapel. So they opened the chapel (it was late at night), and brought in a light to look for him . . . And there, sure enough, he was, sitting in his confession-box in the dark, wide awake, and laughing like softly to himself. Then they knew something was wrong."

"God rest his soul!"

The revision attends to this ending in a couple of ways. A chalice is introduced earlier (in place of a rosary), when the body is viewed at the wake: "There he lay, solemn and copious, vested as for the altar, his large hands loosely retaining a chalice." This serves as foreshadowing for an ending that has been elongated as follows:

"It was that chalice he broke. . . . That was the beginning of it. Of course, they say it was all right, that it contained nothing, I mean. But still. . . . They say it was the boy's fault. But poor James was so nervous, God be merciful to him!"

"And was that it?" said my aunt. "I heard something . . ."

Eliza nodded.

"That affected his mind," she said. "After that he began to mope by himself, talking to no one and wandering about by himself. So one night he was wanted for to go on a call and they couldn't find him anywhere.

They looked high up and low down; and still they couldn't see a sight of him anywhere. So then the clerk suggested to try the chapel. So then they got the keys and opened the chapel and the clerk and Father O'Rourke and another priest that was there brought in a light for to look for him. . . . And what do you think but there he was, sitting up by himself in the dark in his confession-box, wide-awake and laughing-like softly to himself?"

She stopped suddenly as if to listen. I too listened; but there was no sound in the house: and I knew that the old priest was lying still in his coffin as we had seen him, solemn and truculent in death, an idle chalice on his breast.

Eliza resumed:

"Wide-awake and laughing-like to himself. . . . So then, of course, when they saw that, that made them think that there was something gone wrong with him. . . ."

The pause to listen before the repetition of the closing lines slows down the close, obliging the reader to patience, and in the process enhancing tension. True, there's a mild risk of melodrama (accentuated by quoting the passage in isolation) but also a sense of Joyce slowing before the finish line. He knows how and where the story will end—he's already written it in the earlier draft, after all—now he's savoring it, pacing it more deliberately. We might understand expansion as the form patience takes on the page.

Isaac Babel's *Collected Stories* offers an even richer example. His sketch "Information" concerns a callow young man's encounter with an experienced prostitute, Vera. She drags him around the streets and taverns, makes him wait while she eats, chats with a bartender, and even helps an elderly neighbor pack for a trip. His passions cooling, the young client is suddenly inspired to tell her a story—anything to have her *see* him. Preying on her soft heart, he charms her with a made-up tale of depravity—he's a kept "boy," has never been with a woman—and she takes him into her arms as a "fellow" worker, "my little sister." So successfully has he revised himself that in the morning when it comes time to settle she refuses his money, in a sense paying him back for his tale.

The story is barely four pages long, a wry, lively anecdote of the demimonde, but somewhat skeletal. Its single-mindedness is hinted at by the way it "sticks the landing," ending on a punch line—"my first fee"—which Babel took as the title of its later revision, though notably he wisely writes "through" this earlier ending, if not quite burying the title line at least throwing a little dirt over it in the penultimate paragraph.

"My First Fee" is twice the length of "Information," and much of the extra space is devoted to the narrator's character. His motivations are deepened, his character, previously generic, more defined. Whereas in the earlier version his sexual desire is a given, now when we meet him his hunger has added edge. He is, as he tells us ruefully, "renting a room in the attic from a newlywed Georgian couple . . . [who] in the grip of love thrashed about like two large fish trapped in a jar." Babel's characteristic surreal poetry—here put to comic effect—is more evident in this draft. "At night," his narrator goes on to note with deadpan piteousness, "the thumping and babbling of my neighbors was followed by a silence as piercing as the whistle of a cannonball." (For all that I'm using Babel here as an exemplar of narrative expansion, *stylistically* he prized concision— "Your language becomes clear and strong, not when you can no longer add a sentence, but when you can no longer take away from it"—which surely contributes to his poetic compression of imagery.)

The narrator's backstory is also drawn in more detail. In the earlier version, we know the narrator is a writer. It begins as if in response to a letter from a reader or fellow writer: "In answer to your inquiry, I would like to inform you that I set out on my literary career early in life, when I was about twenty. I was drawn to writing by a natural affinity, and also by my love for a woman named Vera."

The setup is confident, even complacent, promising both the anecdote and the career to come. But in the revision we sense something more tenuous. The narrator is "working as a proofreader for the printing press of the Caucasus Military District" and his aspirations to the literary life seem frustrated, even burdensome:

> Since childhood, I had invested every drop of my strength in creating tales, plays, and thousands of stories. They lay on my heart like a toad on a stone. Possessed by demonic pride, I did not want to write them down too soon. I felt that it was pointless to write worse than Tolstoy.

The mention of pride promises a subtle new trajectory for the story, albeit a familiar one, the story of pride—in this case literary preciousness—humbled. The pretentious aesthete, who can only be bothered if he can be as good as Tolstoy (a type some of us may recognize), is prompted to spin a yarn for the basest, most human of reasons, and in doing so realizes the power of story (though it's not a cure for writer's block one would recommend for everyone!). Notably, compared to the original anecdote, which could be read as the protagonist putting one over on Vera, the revision suggests that the humorous target is the narrator's younger self. We—now directly addressed midway through as "dear reader"—don't escape the gentle satire either. The story may be called "My First Fee," but Vera is also described as the narrator's "first reader," reminding us that we're also implicated in his narrative seductions (*dear* reader, indeed).

The story, as we might expect, includes several insights about writing, most memorably, perhaps, "A well-thought-out story doesn't need to resemble real life. Life itself tries with all its might to resemble a well-crafted story," a line that might make us wonder who has been lied to—Vera (neatly named, we realize belatedly) or ourselves?

In its subtleties, this version, in fact, echoes one of Babel's most famous stories, "Guy de Maupassant," which sees yet another starving artist type using literature as seduction, albeit in rather different circumstances. The amorous focus is now a genteel middle-class wife whom the writer is being paid to help translate Maupassant, and the reversal of financial power underlines that it is now he who is in a sense prostituting himself. "Guy de Maupassant" is the story that contains Babel's most often quoted lines of writing advice, advice that might seem especially pertinent to revision.

Most famous might be: "No iron can stab the heart with such force as a period put just at the right place." (Raymond Carver thought that line "ought to go on a three-by-five" over his desk and paired it with a wry

observation of Evan Connell's: "he knew he was finished with a short story when he found himself going
through it and taking out commas and then going
through the story again and putting commas back in the
same places.")

Still, the line of Babel's that might be most pertinent
to our subject, again from "Guy de Maupassant," is:

> A phrase is born into the world good and bad at the
> same time. The secret rests in a barely perceptible
> turn. The lever must lie in one's hand and get warm.
> It must be turned once, and no more.

That may be true of a phrase, especially in the hands
of a genius like Babel, but if we were to paraphrase
and say "a *draft* is born into the world good and bad
at the same time," the examples of "Information" and
"My First Fee" (and "Guy de Maupassant") suggest that
several cranks of the lever may be required, or at least
that we might let it lie a long time warming in the
hand. Poignantly, Babel himself was ultimately denied
that time. His last recorded words in Soviet custody
before his execution: "I am asking for only one thing—
let me finish my work." (Babel's own end is subject to a
poignant revision in *The Archivist's Story*, a novel by a
former student of mine, Travis Holland, which imagines into existence one of Babel's confiscated manu-

scripts. My own small revisionary contribution to *The Archivist's Story*: encouraging Travis to *name* his balding bespectacled prisoner after the writer he was so clearly modeled on.)

A more recent example of wonderful revisionary expansion is provided by Carmen Maria Machado's story "The Husband Stitch," a story that itself sets out to revise and expand a preexisting tale, the folktale or urban legend called "The Green Ribbon," which Machado first read in a children's book, *In a Dark, Dark Room and Other Scary Stories*, by Alvin Schwartz (author of the Scary Stories to Tell in the Dark series). The Schwartz version, itself drawing on earlier antecedents, follows a female protagonist, Jenny, who wears a mysterious green ribbon around her neck, from girlhood through marriage to old age, when she finally allows her curious husband to untie the ribbon, with macabre consequences. Machado has modestly described her early draft as a "straight re-telling" of the original, though that shortchanges her significant additions to the children's story—the experiences of passion, pregnancy, birth, and motherhood among them. The brilliant final draft included in her 2017 collection *Her Body and Other Parties* goes further still—swelling to include a slew of other folktales (of brides and mothers and old women, mirroring the protagonist's life journey), and to incorporate a recurring direct address featuring instructions for how to read the story (a trope Machado also traces back to Schwartz's work, as well as the oral tradition of campfire stories). The effect is to grow the story into a kind of compendium of folktales, echoing the form of classic volumes by Charles Perrault and the Brothers Grimm, and to grant it a sly self-consciousness of its relation to those earlier tales. The result is a final draft profoundly wise to its own lineage (as befits a story in part about motherhood), and a reminder of revisionary expansion as the work of fertile imagination.

I'm stressing the values of expansion here in the face of several ingrained biases against it. Writers, of course, are wary of writing long for fear of boring a reader. None of us wants to be called long-winded or verbose, let alone self-indulgent. By contrast, we're reminded that "less is more," that "brevity is the soul of wit," and so we aspire to economy. There's much to be said for these values—though it's worth noting that they're perhaps most relevant to short fiction, the form many of us first adopt—but they can also unconsciously constrain and even limit our imaginative work.

To focus on one such bias and its effect on revision, imagine a spectrum of criticism running from "incomprehensible" to "obvious." At one end of this scale a story is so opaque, so mysterious as to be essentially illegible; at the other, the story is all too predictably and dully legible. For any given story there's some notional sweet spot where the balance of mystery and clarity is just right (a balance that lies not only in the story, but also in the relationship between an individual reader and the story). Early drafts tend not to land on this sweet spot immediately, and revision is thus in part a question of recalibration or range-finding. What's noticeable, though, in many early drafts that I see is a tendency to fall short of the sweet spot rather than to overshoot it, a tendency that may derive from our critical language. Most writers after all prefer to be told that their work is "too subtle"—too much of a good thing (if it's possible to have too much of something understated)—rather than "heavy-handed" and as a result we err on the side of mystery, ambiguity, opacity (all of which have some positive connotations) rather than on the side of the obvious, or explicit (perhaps if we called these things lucidity or frankness the bias might be redressed).

There's likely also something defensive at work here. If my work is opaque to you, that's a criticism, but a softened one—softened precisely by the knowledge (an *admission* on the critic's part) that you don't fully understand it. And how can you truly criticize it if you didn't get it? Our common lot as readers and students of literature invariably includes some experience of *not* getting a classic work; incomprehension is thus easily mistaken as handmaiden to genius.

I should say I sympathize with this defensiveness, or at least its root cause. Our anxiety in sharing work is an index of how much we care about the work. It's that care that makes us so chary of criticism, and yet without it we'd never undertake revision. And revision may well be the surest way to draw the sting of criticism. If we understand what we're sharing as only one draft of many, after all, part of a process, not its end point, feedback is easier both to hear and to act upon.

There remains a danger in our bias toward subtlety, though. It may make the calibration and range-finding of revision harder if we persistently err on one side of the sweet spot. The first draft is too subtle, the next is just slightly less subtle, and so on and so on, resulting in what I think of as Zeno's revision, after the famous paradox. Zeno suggests that if we travel halfway to a destination—like an arrow toward a target, say—and then halfway again, and then halfway *again*, we never actually arrive at our destination. Some might say, despairingly, that *all* revision is Zeno's revision, since it feels as if we continuously approach and yet never quite reach an end point, though I hope to offer an ending to this story of revision in due course. In the meantime, I'd suggest that a way to correct for an overabundance of subtlety in one draft is to *overcorrect*, to consciously allow for heavy-handedness, in the next. It's possible the next draft too will miss the mark, but by overshooting, and that failed experiment provides useful data, since we now know our sweet spot lies somewhere *between* our drafts.

This concept of calibration can be applied more broadly to the revision process. Subsequent drafts often overcorrect for previous ones, swinging back and forth, foresight giving way to hindsight, until—hopefully—we finally hone in on the just-right Goldilocks draft.

One further example of expansionary possibility.

Critics (in workshop, say) are often very effective at identifying problems in a story, and a natural response to such feedback is to cut those problems: the scene that doesn't work, the character who isn't plausible, the odd distracting details. We lop off these sore thumbs, hammer flat these proud nails. But what are we left with? The result of this kind of revision—call it premature editing—can be a story that doesn't do anything glaringly wrong, but that also might not do very much right.

Often, in fact, it's exactly these odd details, these untidy anomalies, that are worth expanding upon. The things in a story that seem easiest to cut are the things of which we say *I'm not even sure why that's there*, which is to say they may be the least planned, most alive things, the places where our subconscious is breaking through our conscious intent. Following those leads, rather than erasing them, is a good way to make the kind of discoveries we're seeking.

A fascinating example of the interrogation of an apparently incongruous or even superfluous detail can be found in a pair of Flannery O'Connor stories. "The Geranium" and "Judgement Day" were her first and last published stories, respectively, and serve as provocative bookends to her *Complete Stories*, posthumous winner of the National Book Award in 1972. The former piece first appeared in 1946 and was the title story of O'Connor's master's thesis at the Iowa Writers' Workshop the following year. The latter, from 1964, is the final story in her collection *Everything That Rises Must Converge* and clearly a revision of the former albeit at a remove of almost two decades (intermediate drafts, one from 1954 entitled "An Exile in the East" also exist, as noted by Robert Giroux in his introduction to the *Complete Stories*). Both versions concern an old and ailing white Southerner brought to live with his daughter in a New York City tenement (the first version predates O'Connor's own six-month stint in NYC in 1949, though she had visited the city as a tourist in 1943). He pines for home, and specifically a compliant Black companion (part friend, part servant, part stereotype), and each story is catalyzed by the moving into the next-door apartment of an African American couple.

There are important differences between the stories. The close of "Judgement Day" is much harsher. The old man, Tanner, who has been dreaming of shipping his own coffin back to the South, dies at the end (the earlier version only anticipates its character's death in the image of the titular potted geranium, which ends up smashed "at the bottom of the alley with its roots in the air"). Such escalation is a familiar revisionary intensification, though the move in this case may also partly reflect O'Connor's own sense of mortality in the final months before she succumbed to lupus. The story was sent to Robert Giroux only a month before her death, and there's poignancy in the idea of O'Connor—a writer described by her teacher Paul Engle as "constantly revising, and in every case improving," who once said of herself, "No one can convince me I shouldn't rewrite as much as I do"—revising to the very last.

Still, while the stories clearly share a premise and the broad outlines of a central action, certain images take on startlingly complex new life in the later version.

In the former, say, we find this piece of callous minstrelsy (the old man is called Dudley in this version):

> Niggers don't think they're dressed up till they got
> on glasses, Old Dudley thought. He remembered
> Lutish's glasses. She had saved up thirteen dollars
> to buy them. Then she went to the doctor and asked

him to look at her eyes and tell her how thick to get the glasses. He made her look at animals' pictures through a mirror and he stuck a light through her eyes and looked in her head. Then he said she didn't need any glasses. She was so mad she burned the corn bread three days in a row, but she bought her some glasses anyway at the ten-cent store. They didn't cost her but $1.98 and she wore them every Saddey. "That was niggers," Old Dudley chuckled.

This racist "comedy" at the expense of Lutish, the cook at Old Dudley's boardinghouse, is deliberately deployed by O'Connor. The patronizing lampooning of a Black person "putting on airs," as Dudley might say, is in marked contrast to the enraged confusion he feels when his dapper new African American neighbor helps him upstairs, pats him on the back, and calls him "old timer." Still, the detail of the glasses itself feels a little arbitrary. It lacks the blunt reality of more familiar stereotypes—Dudley by his own bigoted lights may even intend it affectionately—but its sheer eccentricity makes its use as a generality seem forced. A workshop or an editor (even in 1946) might suggest cutting it, especially as Lutish, the wife of Rabie, Dudley's fishing companion, seems a secondary figure.

Still, the image of glasses—so suggestive of new seeing, re-vision—is retained in "Judgement Day," albeit in far stranger, more elaborate form. Once again, the older white protagonist—now just named Tanner (the faux affectionate sobriquet "old" has been dropped)—is recalling an encounter in the South, but the flashback is much more involved. He's supervising a crew at a sawmill, something he habitually does with a knife in hand, whittling, both to disguise the fact that he has the shakes and to suggest violence, when a newcomer appears: "A large black loose-jointed Negro, twice his own size, had begun hanging around the edge of the saw mill, watching the others work and when he was not watching, sleeping, in full view of them." Provoked by what he perceives as this idle insolence, Tanner warily approaches the interloper:

> The Negro's eyes were small and bloodshot. Tanner supposed there was a knife on him somewhere that he would as soon use as not. His own penknife moved, directed solely by some intruding intelligence that worked in his hands. He had no idea what he was carving, but when he reached the Negro, he had already made two holes the size of half dollars in the piece of bark.
>
> The Negro's gaze fell on his hands and was held. His jaw slackened. His eyes did not move from the knife tearing recklessly around the bark. He watched as if he saw an invisible power working on the wood.

He looked himself then and, astonished, saw the connected rims of a pair of spectacles.

He held them away from him and looked through the holes past a pile of shavings and on into the woods to the edge of the pen where they kept their mules.

"You can't see so good, can you, boy?" he said and began scraping the ground with his foot to turn up a piece of wire. He picked up a small piece of haywire; in a minute he found another, shorter piece and picked that up. He began to attach these to the bark. He was in no hurry now that he knew what he was doing. When the spectacles were finished, he handed them to the Negro. "Put these on," he said. "I hate to see anybody can't see good."

There was an instant when the Negro might have done one thing or another, might have taken the glasses and crushed them in his hand or grabbed the knife and turned it on him. He saw the exact instant in the muddy liquor-swollen eyes when the pleasure of having a knife in this white man's gut was balanced against something else, he could not tell what.

The Negro reached for the glasses. He attached the bows carefully behind his ears and looked forth. He peered this way and that with exaggerated so-lemnity. And then he looked directly at Tanner and grinned, or grimaced, Tanner could not tell which, but he had an instant's sensation of seeing before him a negative image of himself, as if clownishness

and captivity had been their common lot. The vision
failed him before he could decipher it.

It does indeed feel like a vision, the prompting of
"some intruding intelligence" or "invisible power," so
much more mysterious and cryptic and therefore characteristic of O'Connor (it reminds me ineluctably of another "prosthetic," the artificial leg Manley Pointer steals
from Joy/Hulga in "Good Country People") than the
detail from the earlier draft and yet somehow spring-
ing from it. The former purports to be about Lutish,
but tells us more by contrast about Dudley, emphasiz-
ing their distance; the latter seems more confrontational
than affectionate, but ends up drawing Tanner and
Coleman, his eventual companion, together in common
human mystery. There's a flicker of shared humanity, a
vision heartbreakingly blinked away at the last. Notably,
the expansion is partly facilitated by another edit. Lutish
or an equivalent intermediary is gone and the detail of
the glasses has been remade to directly link Tanner and
Coleman (who has taken on the role of Rabie from the
earlier version).

There are other changes both deft and stark in
"Judgement Day" I might mention, not least O'Connor's
substitution of "Negro" in the 1964 story for the offensive pejorative in the 1946 version (a term O'Connor
used herself in correspondence). The former itself, the
term used by Dr. King in his "I Have a Dream" speech

in 1963, is now considered dated and offensive, an instance of the social and political revision of language that extends beyond that of a single author and their work. More profoundly, a sense of O'Connor's own complicated and conflicted response to those changes over the course of her lifetime may also be glimpsed in the action and tenor of the later story. While Dudley, in the earlier version, for instance, resents the offered helping hand of his Black neighbor, Tanner's plea to the equivalent figure to "Hep me up" is now angrily rejected. He meets his end, instead, head thrust through the rails of a banister, from which his body must be cut free. The image explicitly evoked—a nod back to the title—is one of "a man in the stocks"—a punishment often meted out to slaves. While Tanner is arguably granted the smallest measure of mercy—in a coda, his daughter relents and ships his body home—this may be an instance of revision as reckoning, for character and perhaps even author. Visiting New York City for the first time as a teenager, three years before publishing "The Geranium," O'Connor herself was unsettled by signs of integration, and as late as 1964, the year she wrote "Judgement Day," confessed herself "an integrationist on principle and a segregationist by taste." Still, no dying writer—least of all one with such a stark relationship with faith—calls their last story "Judgement Day" lightly.

Darlings

While Flannery O'Connor's example suggests the value of holding on to and interrogating the kind of anomalous details that don't do enough work in early drafts, there are also those cherished elements we resist cutting that should probably go.

Ben Lerner describes one such instance in his autofiction *10:04* concerning a short story of his, "The Golden Vanity," that appeared in the *New Yorker*. He relates its conception and shares an extract of an early draft— "the prose I generated first, the kernel of the work"— detailing a plot to fake letters from famous writers that the protagonist hopes to sell to an archive. And yet, once the story is tentatively accepted, the editors at the *New Yorker* request "a major cut: to get rid of the stuff about the fabricated correspondence, the section I considered the story's core." Lerner is righteously outraged, refuses to make the edit, and withdraws the story in high dudgeon . . . only to comically climb down off his high horse when friends he trusts concur with the editors' opinion.

What's being described here, so frankly and self-deprecatingly captured by Lerner, is the way we cling to our old hypotheses. Those elements that come early in a story, that essentially *enable* us to write it, are often the hardest to give up. Indeed, *10:04* itself is in part a book about expanding "The Golden Vanity" into a novel—the very novel we're reading!—during the course of which the faked correspondence is briefly restored as a plot point.

I'm inclined to think of elements like this as scaffolding—aspects of a draft as essential to its writing as a scaffold is to the construction of a building—that can be taken down after the story is built. And indeed, much of the expansionary process of revision I have described does eventually give way to a phase of contraction, of cuts and edits. Having expanded the story, we can finally be sure of what we know about it and then allow ourselves to follow Hemingway's advice and "leave out" (or take down) some of the knowledge that allowed it to be constructed.

I use the word *scaffolding* above, but the more familiar term for these props and crutches may be *darlings*. Our dogged resistance to cutting them underlies the single most famous piece of revisionary advice there is: *kill your darlings*. A line so famous as to have a dozen fathers and mothers (among them Faulkner, Wilde, Welty, and Woolf—whose rather chilling variation was "kill your little darlings"). The earliest use of the phrase, though, seems to come from the early-twentieth-century British writer Sir Arthur Quiller-Couch and his 1914 lecture "On Style" warning against "extraneous ornament":

> If you here require a practical rule of me, I will present you with this: "Whenever you feel an impulse to perpetrate a piece of exceptionally fine writing, obey it—whole-heartedly—and delete it before sending your manuscript to press. *Murder your darlings.*"

(Note that even here, at the origin of this most famous of all pieces of editorial advice, the impulse toward expansion is still encouraged *before* cutting.)

While Quiller-Couch is barely remembered today, I've been familiar with him, in name at least, almost from the start of my writing life, when I won a prize named after him at college (one of the first encouragements I received as a writer, worth far more in validation than the twenty-five-pound award it came with). So perhaps I might, respectfully, offer a counter to his famous, murderous advice and suggest that writers rather *save your darlings*.

There are various ways to mean this. One could imagine a revisionary strategy that works in a Marie Kondo–like fashion by throwing out everything that doesn't "spark joy," essentially a revision that murderously cuts everything *except* one's darlings. And many writers do employ strategies like this. Philip Roth, in his *Paris Review* interview, describes something similar:

> I often have to write a hundred pages or more before there's a paragraph that's alive. Okay, I say to myself, that's your beginning, start there; that's the first paragraph of the book. I'll go over the first six months of work and underline in red a paragraph, a sentence, sometimes no more than a phrase, that has some life in it, and then I'll type all these out on one page. Usually it doesn't come to more than one page, but if I'm lucky, that's the start of page one.

Still, in my own experience, this saving of darlings means something else. While I do often cut them, I resist the urge to kill them and instead try to save them, not in the story, but in a file of ideas, of phrases, of "off-cuts" in case I might find a later use for them. Different writers have different names for this file. Benjamin Percy calls it his "cemetery folder" (appropriately enough for our "undead" darlings); others deem it a "compost heap." Personally, I like to think of it as a lifeboat, or a raft. God, after all, may have sent the Flood to revise his work, but he too saved the best bits of his first draft in the Ark.

And what becomes of all these darlings? What are we saving them for?

To call on another metaphor, a trick of the mind I deploy in these cases is the idea of the jigsaw puzzle. For the sake of argument, let's say it's a picture of a desert island. Often, we pick up the wrong piece of the puzzle—blue, but is it the sky or the sea?—and try to jam it into the corner we're working on before realizing it doesn't fit. But at that point we set it aside. We don't throw it away. We hope and assume it will find its rightful place in some other part of the puzzle. The piece is a "darling," the puzzle is the totality of our writing, not just this one story, but a lifetime of writing. And every so often one of these stray darlings, cut months or years before from one story, will find its proper home in another.

Dan Chaon speaks of such a process as he assembled his collection, aptly titled in this context, *Among the Missing*:

> It's weird to look back at old drafts and see that Sandi in "Safety Man" once suffered from the unexplained blackouts that now plague the narrator of "Big Me," and that the blow-up doll in "Safety Man" actually first made his appearance as a brief image in "Falling Backwards."

This movement of "pieces" from story to story can also apply between novels and stories. The trans character

Reese in Brit Bennett's outstanding 2020 novel, *The Vanishing Half*, for example, began as a figure called Reece in a story she workshopped with me in 2012. Similarly, two or three sections cut from my own novel *The Welsh Girl*, had afterlives as short stories; works that I think of as "Teflon" or "Velcro" stories, after those apocryphal "spin-offs" of the space program.

Any discussion of expansion and cutting, and the related dialectic between revision and editing, wouldn't be complete without a consideration of the examples of Raymond Carver's stories as edited by Gordon Lish. As I noted earlier, certain pairs of Carver stories—notably "The Bath" (published in 1981's *What We Talk About When We Talk About Love*) and "A Small, Good Thing" (from *Cathedral* in 1983)—are often cited in textbooks and taught together as examples of revision.

Both stories concern a boy, Scotty, injured in a hit-and-run accident just before his eighth birthday and his parents' subsequent vigil at his hospital bedside. But while "The Bath" ends with the boy's fate and the source of a series of mysterious and menacing phone calls to the family home unresolved, "A Small, Good Thing," almost three times longer, expands and extends its narrative, confirming both the boy's fate and the identity of the caller. He turns out to be a baker commissioned to make a cake for Scotty's birthday that in the crisis the mother has forgotten to pick up. In a final, lengthy scene the grieving parents confront the baker and, contrite, he offers the small comfort of the title in breaking bread with them.

Given this expansion, and the publication order of the versions, it's a natural assumption to consider "A Small, Good Thing" a revision. Certainly contemporary reviews of *Cathedral* made much of the development. Jonathan Yardley in the *Washington Post* began his review by quoting Carver himself on revision:

> I like to mess around with my stories. I'd rather tinker with a story after writing it, and then tinker some more, changing this, changing that, than have to write the story in the first place. That initial writing just seems to me the hard place I have to get to in order to go on and have fun with the story. Rewriting for me is not a chore—it's something I like to do. I think by nature I'm more deliberate and careful than I am spontaneous, and maybe that explains something. . . . Maybe I revise because it gradually takes me into the heart of what the story is about. I have to keep trying to see if I can find that out.

Yardley continued:

> Carver, like all accomplished writers of short stories, understands the importance of leaving things out; but here he demonstrates that he also understands

the importance of putting things in, of exploring a story to the fullest.

Yardley, and several other contemporary critics, ascribed the revision to a shift in Carver's aesthetic, a welcome (to them) move beyond minimalism. Others have gone so far as to attribute the changes in Carver's work around this time to changes in his life—his new sobriety, marriage to Tess Gallagher, and success.

This career narrative, however, has itself become subject to revision since the late 1990s. D. T. Max, in an article entitled "The Carver Chronicles," followed up on scholarly suspicions and literary gossip about Gordon Lish's editorial influence on Carver by examining Lish's papers at Indiana University. What he concluded was a reversal of the conventional wisdom— namely, that "A Small, Good Thing" was in fact an *earlier* version of the story that Lish cut drastically to form "The Bath," a move in keeping with his long-established editorial practice. As Max notes: "In the case of Carver's 1981 collection, *What We Talk About When We Talk About Love*, Lish cut about half the original words and rewrote 10 of the 13 endings." Given this latter suggestion— "Entire paragraphs have been added," Max asserts; "Lish loved deadpan last lines, and he freely wrote them in"— there's even a case that the stories are revisions by another hand.

It's clear from their correspondence that Carver was troubled by these changes, but also conflicted. In one anguished letter to Lish he wrote:

> Gordon, God's truth, and I may as well say it out now, I can't undergo the kind of surgical amputation and transplant that might make [the stories] someway fit into the carton so the lid will close. There may have to be limbs and heads of hair sticking out.

Yet elsewhere he also acknowledges Lish's editorial gifts:

> I see what it is that you've done, what you've pulled out of it, and I'm awed and astonished, startled even, with your insights.

and

> Everything considered, it's a better story now than when I first mailed it your way—which is the important thing, I'm sure.

Some of this ambivalence is doubtless rooted in his long relationship with Lish. They'd known each other since the late 1960s, and when Lish became fiction editor at *Esquire* he accepted (and edited) Carver's first story for a "slick." That Carver was grateful, that he trusted his

friend—a fellow writer and teacher as well as a distin-
guished editor—seems clear. His openness to editing
likely goes back even before Lish to his apprenticeship
with John Gardner as a writing student. In his essay
"John Gardner: Writer and Teacher," Carver recalled
those days as follows:

> Before our conference [Gardner] would have marked
> up my story, crossing out unacceptable sentences,
> phrases, individual words, even some of the punc-
> tuation; and he gave me to understand that these
> deletions were not negotiable. . . . And he wouldn't
> hesitate to add something to what I'd written—a word
> here and there, or else a few words, maybe a sentence
> that would make clear what I was trying to say.

Still, for all the well-documented instances of Lish's
editorial interventions, and the corrective posthumous
publication of Carver's earlier variants (notably in
Beginners, the original manuscript of *What We Talk
About When We Talk About Love*), it's worth noting that
during his lifetime Carver himself only chose to reprint
three stories in his "versions" in *Where I'm Calling From*,
his 1988 volume of "new and selected stories": "A Small,
Good Thing," "So Much Water So Close to Home," and
"Distance."

His decision to reinstate those earlier drafts paradoxically amounts to another form of revision, and makes these three pieces of particular interest to us. Revision, as previously noted, is the sum of what changes *and* what stays the same. And the ability to return to an earlier version is an important revisionary skill—a recognition that we've picked the wrong door, overshot the mark, but also perhaps a tantalizing glimmer of what it means to be done with revision. (It's worth noting at this point that while Carver's versions of these stories predate the Lish versions, they're by no means early drafts. Carver is on record as saying, "I've done as many as twenty or thirty drafts of a story. Never less than ten or twelve drafts.")

Interestingly, the three stories share several overlapping preoccupations. Each concerns a couple with a single child, each is death-haunted. Where "A Small, Good Thing" grapples with the death of the couple's child, "So Much Water So Close to Home" revolves around the husband's chance discovery of the body of a young woman—someone else's child—on a fishing trip. The husband and his buddies don't report the body until they've enjoyed their sport, and this callousness opens a rift between husband and wife. The parallels to their own child, Dean, the titular "closeness to home," is touched upon in both the Lish version ("For a crazy instant I think something's happened to Dean") and the Carver one (there Dean asks to go swimming and the story ends with the wife's accusing, "For God's sake, Stuart, she was only a child").

"Distance" is a quieter story—a father tells a grown daughter of a moment early in his failed marriage to her mother when the daughter was a newborn—but still shadowed by death. The young father in this case plans to go hunting geese with an older friend (a father figure himself) but decides, reluctantly, to stay home when the baby has a fever. The hunting trip feels like an echo of the fishing excursion in "So Much Water So Close to Home," and the resolution—the young wife makes her husband a peace offering of pancakes— reminds us of the coming together over food in "A Small, Good Thing," albeit that the young man in "Distance" spills the pancakes into his lap by accident (hence the title of the Lish variant: "Everything Stuck to Him"), suggesting that food won't be enough to keep the couple together.

Lish's edits of all three pieces also share several similarities. Lish, as Max notes, "was constantly on guard against what he saw as Carver's creeping sentimentality" and this likely accounts for his paring away of the scene with the baker at the end of "The Bath." Somewhere in back of that scene, behind even the allusion to Holy Communion, there's an awkward echo of the pregnancy euphemism "a bun in the oven," of which Lish may have been wary. Certainly, he also, and probably rightly, cut a heavy-handed reference to geese mating for life from "Everything Stuck to Him" (though that title suggests Lish wasn't above some clunkiness himself). Lish's laconicism—so central to Carver's trademark minimalism—is also much in evidence in these drafts, though at times the trademark seems less Carver's or even Lish's than Hemingway's. In "Distance," say, we read: "A few minutes later the baby began to cry once more, and this time they both got up, and the boy swore." In "Everything Stuck to Him," however, Lish seems to be channeling Hemingway in his terse "The boy did a terrible thing. He swore."

That shadow of Hemingway might also explain another similarity between the edited versions of "The Bath" and "So Much Water So Close to Home." Both essentially suppress female agency. In "A Small, Good Thing," for instance, it's the mother who figures out the identity of the caller and initiates the climactic confrontation: "It came to her then. She knew who it was. Scotty, the cake, the telephone number. She pushed the chair away from the table and got up. 'Drive me down to the shopping center,' she said." Once they're there, she also takes the lead. She's clearly angry, but "She knew she was in control of it, of what was increasing in her. She was calm." And this combination of rage and calm—"'I know bakers work at night,' Ann said. 'They make phone calls at night, too. You bastard'"; "'I wanted to kill you,' she said. 'I wanted you dead'"—is one of the things that makes the close so cathartic.

In "So Much Water So Close to Home" the change is, if anything, even starker and more intentional. In Carver's version the wife slaps her husband, pulls away when he tries to initiate sex, makes up a bed for herself on the sofa, and ultimately moves "into the extra bedroom." Lish's version by contrast tends to lay the emphasis on her husband's menace. The girl he's found has been raped, and his own potential for sexual violence is hinted at throughout. Instead of being slapped, he warns his wife not to "rile" him, she continues to share his bed only "lying on the far side . . . away from his hairy legs" and, at the close, acquiesces dully to his sexual advances. The effect is powerful, chilling, but also distinct from the female anger and judgment that both the baker in "A Small, Good Thing" and the husband in Carver's version of "So Much Water So Close to Home" quail before. There's a sense here, then, that the edits also reflect a different narrative emphasis, not simply a distillation of the originals, maybe even a different sensibility between author and editor.

For all this, what makes Lish's edits so compelling is that on a line-by-line basis they're often spot-on. Max describes them as "like the expert cropping of a picture" and I'm inclined to agree, and yet as already noted there's a sense of something intangible being cut, too.

As Stephen King, in his review of Carver's *Collected Stories*, says of "A Small, Good Thing":

> In Carver's version, the couple—who are actually characters instead of shadows—go to see the baker, who apologizes for his unintended cruelty when he understands the situation. . . . This version has a satisfying symmetry that the stripped-down Lish version lacks, but it has something more important: it has *heart*.

Heart—the very thing Carver speaks of seeking in revision, and a glimpse perhaps of the beating whole that is more than the sum of the parts of revision.

I still teach these pairings in class; I find them if anything more illuminating now that we better understand their relationship. My practice is typically to present "A Small, Good Thing" as it was originally understood, as a revision of "The Bath," and discuss it briefly in that light, and then to reverse course and "reveal" the editorial relationship. The trick tends to make for a richer conversation. In the first instance a kind of teleological inevitability limits debate in much the same way that published work is often less "open" to discussion than student work. Basically, the students assume Carver knew what he was doing and his revisionary choices are justified by his reputation. Reversing the drafts shakes up that dynamic and tends to divide opinion in the room: some prefer one version, some the other. Surely there's some primacy effect in play (and indeed on occasion I assign different people in class to read different versions first) but as the conversation continues, it often becomes clear that individual students like some of Lish's choices and some of Carver's, which echoes my own sense that Lish is a very crisp line editor—he cuts fat from Carver's sentences with surgical precision—and yet the cumulative effect of these cuts is sometimes to throw the baby out with the bathwater. Some human element, as King notes, some sense of individuality and feeling, is sacrificed in the Lish version. It's often said, including by me, that even late drafts usually have 5 to 10 percent "fat" on them—it's less a case of cutting scenes or paragraphs at that stage than of trimming lines, clauses, adverbs—but some fat, it turns out, may actually be good for the heart.

This talk of fat calls to mind some of the underlying metaphors for editing. We talk of trimming it, paring it—evoking images of the butcher's shop, the kitchen. Corresponding mentions of bones ("Cut it to the bone," in Stephen King's words, or "Write a sentence as clean as a bone," in James Baldwin's) are almost as common. Carver's own name, in this sense, is symbolic of his (or perhaps ironically Lish's) style. Our choice of metaphors, as always, reveals something about us. Sometimes we wield a cleaver, or even an axe, emboldening ourselves, but also raising fears of going too far in a revision. Sometimes we wield a scalpel, the surgical echo implying we've taken a kind of Hippocratic oath toward our stories to do no harm in revision. Others reach for images of carpentry ("workshop" often involves a conversation about writing "tools"), still others borrow the language of cooking (I was once warned by a British editor about "over-egging" a story).

As an aside, let's pause here to mark the implicit gender bias to some of these metaphors. Cutting—whether surgery, butchery, or carpentry—can feel very male (as might all that slaughter of darlings). As Nick Hornby says of the winnowing process:

> People are desperate to make [writing] sound like manly, back-breaking labor because it's such a wussy thing to do in the first place. The obsession with austerity is an attempt to compensate, to make writing resemble a real job, like farming, or logging.

By contrast, another of my favorite descriptions of editing, one that reconciles the tension between cutting and expanding a story by hinting at the way editing can *enrich*, draws from the kitchen. It's from Claire Messud:

> In revision, you begin a kind of creative destruction. If you've written three scenes and each of them does a different thing . . . if you could have one scene that would do everything at once that those three scenes are doing, then that would be better. . . . So you compress, the same way that to make something very tasty you might reduce a sauce.

In an interesting postscript, both "A Small, Good Thing" and "So Much Water So Close to Home" are among the several Carver adaptations that have been filmed. Both feature in Robert Altman's 1993 ensemble piece *Short Cuts*, and "So Much Water So Close to Home" is also the basis for the 2006 *Jindabyne*. Both treatments make for fascinating and provocative revisions-by-(yet)-another-hand. *Jindabyne*, in particular, might serve as a kind of counterfactual, what a further expanded revision of "So Much Water So Close to Home" might have looked like if Carver had ever embarked on one.

"So Much Water So Close to Home" features only briefly in *Short Cuts*, a kind of novelistic amalgam of ten Carver pieces. The husband and wife feature as much in other stories as in their own (she is reimagined as a children's clown and shows up at the hospital where Scotty, the boy from "A Small, Good Thing," is taken). But "So Much Water . . ." is given a much more expansive treatment in *Jindabyne*. If the relocation of *Short Cuts* to Los Angeles feels a little "off" for Carver—the makeup artists, motorcycle cops, and painters (not to mention a cameo by Alex Trebek) don't feel quite right—the Australian setting of *Jindabyne* works surprisingly well. The real town of Jindabyne in New South Wales has itself been relocated, its original buildings submerged under a man-made lake. There's thus a sense in the film of a whole community, a whole history having been drowned. Furthermore, the dead girl in this case is Aborigine, and the fishermen who find her are white, which adds a charged social and racial dynamic to the story, another narrative of submergence.

The drama of the filmed version is also heightened in a variety of other ways. In its longer form, the story notes that the wife, Claire, has been subject to psychological challenges as a mother—postpartum depression seems suggested—leading to a period of hospitalization during which time her mother-in-law moved closer to care for Claire's son, Dean. This backstory is absent from the Altman version, which eliminates Dean altogether and seems to take its lead from the Lish version of the story. By contrast, in *Jindabyne* (and Carver's longer draft), the sense is that Claire has temporarily abandoned her son in the past, and now Stuart has abandoned or neglected his duties to another child, the drowned girl. But the movie goes even further in this vein, ramping up the stakes by making Claire newly and ambivalently pregnant again.

These moves are in keeping with a revisionary adaptation that pushes further in almost every respect. The secondary characters—the fishing buddies—are all given more extensive roles. Their friendship and their relationships with their own wives and girlfriends are put under considerable stress. And the echoing threat of drowning is ever present—Dean doesn't know how to swim, but plays in the lake; one scene of Claire swimming is shot from below (as if to evoke the menace of *Jaws*).

The list of these expansions goes on, sometimes exhaustingly—at just over two hours the movie plays a little lugubriously at times—but there are also several moments that deepen and complicate the story. Stuart comes in for considerable additional attention. The moment of the discovery of the body is portrayed as shocking and traumatic for him (in the Altman version, one of the men—not Stuart—finds it while pissing in the river) and makes Stuart rather more sympathetic. Later he offers a rationale—they don't want to take the body out of the water because of the heat, which makes some sense (especially in the Australian setting)—and later still a more feeling explanation of why they continued fishing. "I felt alive," he tells his wife, and we understand that fishing the next day was somehow life-affirming after the grisly discovery. It's an addition, but one that feels in keeping, a touch of the "heart" that King finds in Carver. The changes don't excuse the men's callousness, but rather explain it and remind us that any of us might make the same kind of moral error—notes absent from the original and from the intervening versions by Lish and Altman. Those versions feel like subtractions. *Jindabyne*, by contrast, so interested in the sunken and drowned, illustrates the added depths that a revision can aspire to.

These Carver/Lish examples seem to imply a distinction between revision and editing—different aesthetics, even a tension between expansion and cutting—reminiscent of Thomas Wolfe's famous division of writers into "putter-inners" and "leaver-outers." And yet can't we, shouldn't we, be both? I suspect in fact that these seemingly opposing energies are often complementary, that there's a kind of dialectical relation between them, with rounds of expansion, followed by contraction, followed by further expansion and contraction (another version of our revisionary calibration). It's as if a story or a novel were alive, breathing out and then in, out and then in. The first draft of *The Welsh Girl*, for example, the "kitchen sink" version as I dubbed it, was 550 pages in manuscript, and an unwieldy mess, so much so that the next draft, the "diet" draft, was a skinny 150 pages that revealed the essential, central narrative movement. But I wasn't done there, thanks in large part to an editor and an agent who were more patient than I and encouraged me to add back some of what had been cut until I had my final, Goldilocks draft that came in at around 350 pages.

The cartoonist Nick Drnaso describes an analogous, if darker, trajectory for his searing 2018 graphic novel, *Sabrina*. The story deals with the aftermath of the titular character's abduction and murder, but in earlier drafts of the book Drnaso included depictions of her death, grim scenes he reports having been able to draw only after getting drunk. After completing the book in 2016, however, he began to have second thoughts: "The feeling of having created a fictionalized character that I then murdered for the purpose of a fictional story . . . felt weirdly awful . . . felt like I was weirdly being exploitative of other people's pain and misery." In an interview in the *New Yorker*, he recounts how after the 2016 election of Donald Trump he "began to think that there was no point in putting something like this out in a world that's drowning in negative subject matter," and concluded, "It's not going to be healthy for anyone to read this." He went so far as to withdraw the book from publication, but later relented, choosing to cut the scenes of violence, and instead add moments of grace, including pages in which Sabrina's sister talks of her trauma. In total he took out six pages, and added another thirty. The cuts in this case presaged a significant expansion, and not just in length, but also in the emotional scope and tenor of the book. Revision enlarged the vision of the book, enabling it to see not only more clearly but also further.

Some of the same process is also discernable in a story by Kirstin Valdez Quade (from her luminous debut collection, *Night at the Fiestas*). Kirstin is a former colleague, but even further back I was lucky enough to teach her in a class at the Bread Loaf Writers' Conference, where we workshopped an earlier draft of her story "Mojave Rats." The published version is close in most respects to the already polished and largely realized draft that I saw (one tiny change is that an antagonist, whom I noted in my comments was unnamed, is now called Peter; Kirstin assures me it's not a conscious dig!) but the ending has been decisively revised.

The story concerns Monica, a young mother stranded in a desert trailer park with her two young daughters while her husband, Elliot, conducts fieldwork for his PhD in geology. He's absent for most of the story while Monica struggles with a broken heater and the demands of her children (the elder, Cordelia, child of her first marriage, is bored and tetchy; the younger, Beatrice, is a fussy infant). In a climactic act—half renunciation, half spite—Monica gives away a cocktail dress, a vestige of the more privileged life of her earlier marriage, to a neighbor girl, Amanda.

Elliot returns at the close of both drafts, but in the first he returns with a story: he has seen the body of a naked woman on the highway, victim of a hit-and-run. It's a striking, nightmarish image and one can see the appeal of it to the writer—it evokes Monica's own abandonment and the way she has earlier slipped out of her beautiful dress to give it away—and yet it also feels like too much. The story of the dead woman is a pointed underlining of the story's themes, and yet also seems to compete with the main action (the dead woman's narrative is more luridly dramatic).

Elliot's anecdote is gone from the published draft, but it's less the cut that is striking than the expansion it enables. In the earlier draft Elliot's story brings Amanda back to Monica's mind—she conflates the neighbor girl with the dead woman—so that the emotional attention at the close turns to Amanda. In the published version, it is the daughter Cordelia—a more central figure in Monica's life, and the story—who has an enlarged and more emotionally satisfying role at the close. Cutting Elliot's anecdote—the story inhaling—has thus created space to expand Cordelia's presence—the story exhaling. And this breathing in and out of the story has allowed the writer to locate its heart. We're used to talk of climaxes taking our breath away, or making us catch our breath, but the right ending can also make us exhale, sigh with aesthetic satisfaction.

Just more metaphors, of course. Still, the sense of a draft as a living thing may be more useful, and more hopeful, than the idea of our writing as something to kill and cut up. And as for writers? Separating us into putter-inners and taker-outers makes about as much sense as dividing ourselves into breather-inners and breather-outers.

Dun, Dun . . . Done

The middle of the story of a revision, as I noted earlier, can be a tangle, a recursive process of try and try again, calibrate and recalibrate. But what about the endgame? When we've run the experiments, made the choices, expanded, cut, saved our darlings, rinsed and repeated, how do we know when enough is enough? How do we know when we're done?

I'm getting to that, but in the spirit of fostering patience (or perhaps just creating impatience for the sake of narrative tension) let's go back to the beginning before we get to the end—a handy revisionary tactic since problems late in a story often stem from earlier ones—and specifically to titles.

It's easy to forget to revise titles. They have a tendency to become set in stone very quickly, and because of their brevity, that quality of either working or not, they can seem resistant, even impervious to revision. Much as we struggle to find the right one—perhaps *because* it is such a struggle—they quickly become labels, "givens" that we don't question from draft to draft. Titles remind me of a child's name, in that respect: something debated by parents for months before the birth, which swiftly comes to seem inevitable as soon as it is bestowed (luckily, character names are more flexible or Connie Gustafson might never have become Holly Golightly, an eleventh-hour revision by Truman Capote).

And yet titles are well worth revising. Sometimes we need to move through several bad ones to get to better ones. Sometimes even bad ones can prove useful and revealing. If your story is named for a theme, say, chances are that draft will be thematically driven. If it is named for a setting, an event, or a character, those are likely to be your focus. Early drafts are often named after the climax or even the "point" of a story—dangerous spoilers for readers, but temporary aids to a writer as a kind of map, a reminder of an anticipated destination (more scaffolding, in other words). We can even turn this tendency to our own ends: changing the title of a subsequent draft can serve as a nudge toward a new goal, a new emphasis for the next revision.

Jennifer Egan's illuminating website for her Pulitzer-winning *A Visit from the Goon Squad* shares the draft titles for several stories. "Gold Cure," for instance, was originally "The House of Shame," a thematically suggestive title if ever I heard one; "Ask Me if I Care" was "Class of '79," a setting title; "Found Objects" was "Happy Ending," a destination title (whether sincere or ironic).

The Welsh Girl in its earlier drafts was called *The Bad Shepherd*, a title that I prefer in some ways (and a darling I saved by bestowing it on one of those spin-off stories later), but that obscured, from me, who the central character was. *Gatsby* was reportedly at one point "Hurrah for the Red, White and Blue"—a terrible title, but one within whose crude satirical sarcasm we can read the subtler irony of *The Great Gatsby*. An early version of *Lady Chatterley's Lover* (itself a model title—three words, indicating two main characters, and key tensions: illicit relations and class) was in one draft entitled "John Thomas and Lady Jane"—antique British euphemisms for male and female genitalia respectively. An unworkable, unpublishable, almost *unthinkable* title, but one that I suspect emboldened Lawrence, reminded him daily of his avowed intent to speak forthrightly and frankly about sex.

Published titles come at the start of a story or a book, of course, but often arrive, as these examples suggest, late in revision, so perhaps addressing titles as we approach doneness is not so anti-intuitive.

One familiar version of doneness is exhaustion, or boredom. There are writers who will describe this as the end point of revision, by which measure stories are less finished than abandoned. But boredom seems to me a rather dispiriting end point for a creative process.

That's not to say that boredom isn't part of a writer's lot. As Susan Sontag acknowledged, "The life of the [writer] is led, directed and controlled by boredom."

But as she also noted, "Avoiding boredom is one of our most important purposes."

Boredom, as any child knows, is the soil for day-dreaming, for imagination. Every writer is a writer because they were bored—as a kid, in college, at work. Boredom isn't the end, it's just a phase of the process—often the one right before a breakthrough if we can only outwait it (there's that note of patience again).

Which brings us at last to real doneness, the end of our revisionary story.

As I've suggested—contrary to workshop rules of engagement—we *don't* all know what we intend when we set out on a first draft. Let me stress, this is not some spurious binary between having an intention and not having one. Not knowing what we intend isn't the same as having *no* intention. We do often have some idea, some sense—call it a hypothesis, as I do, call it a hunch, an inkling, what you will—but our writing often reveals to us the limits of that idea, the fuzziness of it.

At which point, of course, we're often tempted to give up. We lose faith in the shining idea that got us started when we discover its flaws. I'd argue on the contrary that we need to persevere, that the discovery we've made—that our idea *isn't* as sharp as we hoped—doesn't mean the idea is no good; rather, it suggests it's more complex, *more* not *less* worthy of further exploration. And that seems to me to be exactly the purpose of revision—not the perfection of the expression of some already known subject or idea, but the investigation and extrapolation of it, toward a deeper understanding.

We revise—which is to say we *write*—to understand our intent, to understand our own stories, to understand ourselves. Since Joyce there's been much, perhaps too much, talk of epiphany in fiction, so much so that it's become a predictable trope for characters and readers to arrive (ideally simultaneously) at a climactic epiphany in a short story. But "doneness" seems a less-remarked-upon epiphany, not one for the character or the reader, but for the writer, though I'd hazard that it may be the primary one, without which characters and readers would be unable to experience their epiphanies. As such, that understanding seems like the climax of the story of revision. Perhaps, understood correctly, writerly obsession with epiphany for our characters and stories is merely a reflection of our own search for this epiphany in composition.

As Updike says, "Writing and rewriting are a constant search for what one is saying."

Or as Didion puts it: "I write entirely to find out what I'm thinking."

And the reason we, like Dorothy Parker, love *having* written—truly written, including revision—is because it means finally understanding what we've been doing. And that's how you know you're done: when you understand why you told your story in the first place, what your intent actually was all along. Doneness by these lights is at once our last and first inspiration, the satisfaction it evokes less perfection than wholeness. And the wholeness of revision, more than the sum of all our changes, is revealed to lie in this understanding.

Let's note, too, that just as epiphany in a story typically changes a character, the epiphany of revision has a similar effect on a writer. All our attention to revising a story, changing it, sharpening it, deepening it . . . and all this time it's been revising us. And herein, perhaps, lies another deep-seated resistance to revision: the change being asked for is not only on the page, but also in us—our vision, our thinking, our understanding. And what are we being changed into? Why, a *writer*! Specifically, the writer of our finally finished story.

By way of example, let me return to my alien abduction story, "The Hull Case." Its beginnings lie generally in my long-standing love of sci-fi and more specifically in the fact that one of the first widely reported abduction cases happened to a mixed-race couple. As the product of a mixed marriage and a member of one, myself, that detail caught my attention. With it came a hunch that the story might be somehow about race (the idea of little gray aliens—neither black nor white— got me further thinking about miscegenation), hence my initial interest in having my characters witness that famous Kirk-Uhura kiss on TV. In the end, the story actually climaxes in a hypnosis session in which the Black husband recalls the details of an experience he's otherwise suppressed. Several of those details I drew from the couple's own account as published at the time, which has since become a kind of template for later abduction lore. They include the now famil-iar tropes of being led, powerless, to a glowing white ship, being naked and subjected to physical examina-tion (genitals, teeth, etc). I had all this settled, written, when—astonishingly belatedly it seems to me now—I realized that I recognized these same tropes from an-other source, that they echoed slave narratives I'd read of the abduction from Africa and slave markets. It struck me with the force of revelation that our cultural obsession with aliens—this was back when *The X-Files* was at the height of its success—is in part a deflection of our anxieties about race, and that the story I'd been writing, which I'd intuited was about race, was *specifi-cally* about slavery and its continuing cultural legacy. It seemed so obvious in retrospect as to make me feel as if the earlier drafts of my story had been "a tale told by an idiot."

The revision that followed, it's worth noting, was very minor, a mere line or two, the addition of an image of snow-covered trees "like great white sails." I didn't need to remake the story and I didn't want to make its subtext explicit. I simply wanted to acknowledge my own comprehension of my story. That I *saw* it. Any changes weren't as important to my sense of completion as my own understanding.

In my memory this is a particularly crisp instance of that "doneness." I can think of a couple more examples of similar revisionary revelations, and other smaller instances of insight abound. Still, it would be a stretch to suggest that I experience this force of revelation with everything I've written (though, having experienced a few such moments, I now write in search of them).

This provokes a question: How rare or common is doneness? That's hard to judge directly since it lies in the eye of the beholder, the writer in this case, but we can glimpse its lack or presence in secondary ways, I think.

Doneness, in some fundamental sense, returns a story to its writer, even if much of the work of revision is to see our work through the eyes of the reader. This is why *I* wrote this. This is what it means to *me*. This is why *I* value it. Knowing that is a powerful justification of the writing act, of the process and the end product, so powerful as to be an end in itself, a goal in itself. Doneness means we're done with the story, and the story is done with us . . . which means that what follows—publication, critical reception, sales, and so on—*aren't* the end goal.

And yet how anxious we are about these things, how obsessed by them, how vulnerable! Those feelings are widespread and deeply human, but also suggest that our work is not often as done as it might be. Doneness, our own sense of it, is a bulwark against such judgments, is in some sense the only judgment that counts. Bringing a work to true completion is to transcend these anxieties, or at the very least to care a little bit less about where the chips fall. So maybe that's the end point of revision, the point at which the opinions of others no longer burden us.

As Jane Smiley advises: "You are striving to read your rough draft analytically and diagnostically. It is neither good or bad. It is simply a work in progress. Judging it is not your job. Understanding it is." She goes on to note this paradox: "As a good reviser you will gain two boons. First, your work will get better, and so will be more likely to get published. Second, you will like doing it so much that you will care less and less about whether it ever gets published."

And just in case this progression toward doneness seems exhausting, compare it to home improvement, as Benjamin Percy does, or even gardening. A lot of people are into DIY, a lot of folks love gardening—especially where I'm from—but personally I can't stand either. All that *work*—weeding, digging, planting, mulching, mowing—and once you're done, you just have to do it all over again next week or month or year. Similarly with home improvement; as any homeowner knows, the place needs to be *re*painted every few years, shingles *re*placed, the roof *re*paired. Revision at least *ends*.

What's exhausting to me is the never ending. *The Welsh Girl* took seven or eight years to write, meaning it's a World War II novel that took longer to write than the war lasted, which is shameful somehow. And yet, in retrospect, it took the time it and I needed to take. I wouldn't be as happy with it if it had taken less time, and indeed while seven or eight years would have seemed an eternity when I set out on the project, if you'd told me four years in that I was halfway it would have been a huge relief. Because in the midst of a novel the real burden is not how long it's taking, but that it might never be done, that it might take forever, and that you might not write anything else ever again. One way to cultivate the patience to arrive at doneness, therefore, may be to contemplate the infinitude of undoneness.

Let me offer one more contemporary example by way of illustrating this progression to doneness.

While Frank O'Connor shifts from close third to first person over the decades of his drafts of "First Confession," Wells Tower proves both a swifter and altogether more radical reviser of point of view as evidenced by published versions of two stories, "On the Show" and "Retreat," from his 2009 collection *Everything Ravaged, Everything Burned*.

The former, first published in *Harper's* in 2007, is a dyspeptically knowing take on the old trope of running away with the circus (and is itself based on a nonfiction piece Tower published in the *Washington Post* in 2000). In this case the runaway is a middle-class college dropout fleeing his unsympathetic stepfather, and the circus a podunk traveling fair, where the protagonist ends up working as a carny on a pirate ship ride (a sourly bathetic echo of the Viking ships in the collection's title story).

The *Harper's* version is told in first person by the young man, but the draft that appears in Tower's collection is told via an omniscient third person, which enters the points of view of a rotating cast of characters. Our previous protagonist—now named Jeff Park—still predominates, but we also get close to other figures glimpsed only on the periphery of the earlier draft, if at all: a young boy molested at the fair; his divorced father; Leon (Jeff's boss on the pirate ride); Gary (another carny); even the judge of a Future Farmers of America contest.

Such a radical revision results in several significant changes. The other point-of-view figures allow the story to slip free of Jeff's passive role as observer-narrator.

The later version opens with the molestation scene, elevating the story's stakes beyond Jeff's own hapless-ness and establishing a queasy mystery (the identity of the molester) that draws the reader on. These inten-sifications of drama are complemented by enhanced emotional and thematic echoes between Jeff's family dynamic (mother and stepfather) and the unfortunate boy's (his divorced dad is on a date at the fair). The omniscience furthermore affords us a better sense of this gaudy, temporary community—the carnies, their marks—a bird's-eye view, one might say, and indeed the story is interested in recurring images of flight and falling (from the passengers on the various rides—one winkingly called the Cliff Hanger—to Jeff being forced to climb fifty feet up an extension ladder to change a bulb).

The story, in this final manifestation, is even wryly self-conscious of its own changes, the way it's been dis-assembled and reassembled into something more sec-tional, or modular. At one point, Jeff's last name, Park, is misheard by his coworker Ellis as Parts, leading Leon to snidely quip, "A hole is better than some of the Parks." It's as if the story has read itself, *which of course it has.*

"On the Show" shares some interesting preoccupations with another story of Tower's from the same collection, "Retreat."

Both have a thematic interest in predation reflected in the striking images of teeth on which both close: a girl's in "On the Show" glow from the phosphorescent candy she's sucking; a forkful of tainted meat slips between them in "Retreat."

Both posit family bonds (Jeff and his mother; two brothers in "Retreat") threatened by an interloper (Jeff's stepfather; a new friend the brothers vie over in "Retreat").

Both even share a saved darling, in the form of a deliberately lame joke cut from one, but inserted in the other. This is from the earlier draft of "Retreat":

> "Baby brother would you like to see a magic trick?"
>
> "Sure," I said.
>
> He picked up an orange from the floor of the truck and held it out to me.
>
> "Feast your eyes on it, touch it. Get the image firmly in your mind. Got it?"
>
> It was a navel orange, flattened slightly on one side.
>
> "Now watch closely," he said, and threw the orange out the window of the truck. "Presto," he said.

This is from the later draft of "On the Show":

> "Want to see *my* magic trick?" Leon says to Jeff Park.
>
> "Yeah, all right."

Leon takes the cigarette from his mouth and taps
a long gray caterpillar of ash onto Jeff Park's shoulder.

"Presto change-o, you're an ashtray."

The joke disappears in one place, reappears somewhere else: a flourish of revisionary sleight of hand!—
but also a hint of the way that, especially as we assemble
a collection of stories, individual pieces provoke changes,
revisions, in one another. (In fact, the joke first appears
almost a decade earlier in the *Washington Post* article
from which "On the Show" descends.)

What the revisions of "Retreat" and "On the Show"
most notably have in common, though, is a ready will-
ingness to shift point of view. In the case of "Retreat,"
the story of two estranged brothers reunited at the
rustic New England retreat of the elder, the shift is
from the younger brother's point of view in the earlier draft to the elder's in the later version. The shift
again intensifies the action. Jeff at the fairground and
the younger brother, Alan, in Maine are both out-
siders: useful observers and natural readerly stand-ins.
Matthew, the elder brother, on the other hand, like
Leon and the carnies at the fair, is more embedded in
his locale, which is also to say more trapped, more desperate. Matthew in particular is ensnared by a kind of
manly, pastoral fantasy that sees him ultimately insist
on eating that mouthful of rotten venison he's hunted.

How much more powerful to read "[I] slipped the fork into my mouth," than "[he] slipped the fork into his mouth"? (Which might remind us of Frank O'Connor's logic earlier.)

The real revelation of this later draft of "Retreat," though, seems like another instance of a story reading itself, understanding itself better. In the later version, Matthew's property includes a little pond he's built by damming a spring behind his house, and at one point the brothers—now named Matthew and Stephen—along with George, the local Matthew has befriended, go for a dip:

> We shed our clothes and pushed off into the pond, each on his own gasping course through the exhilarating blackness of the water. "Oh, oh, oh *God* it feels good," cried Stephen in a voice of such carnal gratitude that I pitied him. But it *was* glorious, the sky and the water of a single world-ending darkness, and we levitated in it until we were as numb as the dead.

Compare this to another famous story's scene of pond swimming:

> Ivan Ivanovitch went outside, plunged into the water with a loud splash, and swam in the rain, flinging his arms out wide. He stirred the water into waves which

set the white lilies bobbing up and down; he swam to the very middle of the millpond and dived, and came up a minute later in another place, and swam on, and kept on diving, trying to touch the bottom.

"Oh, my goodness!" he repeated continually, enjoying himself thoroughly. "Oh, my goodness!" He swam to the mill, talked to the peasants there, then returned and lay on his back in the middle of the pond, turning his face to the rain. Burkin and Alehin were dressed and ready to go, but he still went on swimming and diving. "Oh, my goodness! . . ." he said. "Oh, Lord, have mercy on me! . . ."

There's a deliberate echo here—as in Matthew's willful, delusional "enjoyment" of his own too-gamy game, and the pecking percussion of hammers as the three men put in work on Matthew's new house—of Chekhov's famous story *Gooseberries*, with its own delusional brother who insists on the deliciousness of his homegrown gooseberries, a similarly ecstatic swimming scene and this famously bleak observation:

There ought to be behind the door of every happy, contented man someone standing with a hammer continually reminding him with a tap that there are unhappy people; that however happy he may be, life will show him her claws sooner or later, trouble will come for him.

It's as if between drafts Tower became conscious of the echo—read his own story *and* Chekhov's—owned it, and then put it to use, in a kind of Bloomian revisionary ratio, by both acknowledging the original and ringing a key change on it. Telling the story from the point of view of the delusional brother lays bare his desperation to us, but also—and this is the heartbreaking and pitiless revision enshrined in the point-of-view shift—to *himself.* There's a recognition implicit here, a sense of the story finally knowing itself, that suggests that elusive doneness.

There's a revisionary hesitation I've not touched on yet—call it over-doneness—the anxiety that we might mar a text by over-revising it. While there are shades here of our "first is best" bias, and our "subtlety" bias— the kind of calibration we discussed earlier allows for and even encourages overdoing, with the proviso that what's overdone can always be undone—there are other legitimate concerns about overdoing.

Jesse Lee Kercheval puts her finger on one: "At some point I have to call a halt, and you will too. If you don't, you risk revising a single short story or novel into the many other ones you might have written." The fear here is that a revision can compromise future writing, absorbing or reabsorbing ideas and inspirations that might deserve a separate existence. Obsessive revision in this sense is like some black hole from whose gravity new work can't escape. And there may well be something to this, especially for novels, which are both capacious and a long time in the making. Any writer with work in progress on 9/11 or during the COVID-19 pandemic knows the perils and temptations of incorporating new circumstances into an ongoing project. And yet, I'd argue there's an even greater risk to future work in not revising sufficiently. Those who don't revise are doomed to repeat not only the same mistakes, but also the same *stories*. To be sure, we all have obsessions—recurring themes, say—but these can be expressed in very varied ways. By contrast, if a story remains unfinished we're apt to revisit it—its types and tropes—in the next story, and if that's unfinished, the next and so on and so forth, so that even putatively new stories are revisions, albeit arrested ones, that can't move forward to completion. The result is a kind of temporal loop—call it *Groundhog Day* revision—in which the writer and his or her material remains trapped. Seeing a story through to doneness can thus be a way to break free of the loop, releasing us to tell other stories.

I'm reminded of one of those Hemingway lines with which we started: "I decided that I would write one story about each thing that I knew about." One story. Never mind that Hemingway himself didn't follow his own advice. Never mind that editors and agents and, yes, readers often want us to tell the same successful story multiple times. One story about each thing we know. One story to do it justice. That's a vision of something like wholeness, a vision of doneness.

Yet there remains a lingering fear of doneness, or over-doneness, more subtle, more sophisticated, than the rest: call it an existential anxiety. Wholeness, completion, certainly perfection smack of hubris, after all, even impiety—hence those Oriental rugs with the deliberate mistake woven into them. The Persian flaw acknowledges that only God is perfect.

This existential misgiving reminds me of an idea Robert Boswell articulates in the title essay of his excellent book on writing, *The Half-Known World*:

> I have grown to understand narrative as a form of contemplation, a complex and seemingly incongruous way of thinking. I come to know my stories by writing my way into them. . . . I work from a kind of half-knowledge.
>
> In the drafts that follow, I listen to what has made it to the page. Invariably, things have arrived that I did not invite, and they are often the most interesting things in the story. By refusing to fully know the world, I hope to discover unusual formations in the landscape, and strange desires in the characters. By

declining to analyze the story, I hope to keep it open to surprise.

Following Boswell, we might suggest that we set out to write what we half-know, and my argument is that we revise toward a full knowing. Boswell himself, though, seems a little equivocal in respect of full knowing, writing: "I resist knowing until the story finally rubs my nose in it" (which seems reluctant at best), and elsewhere "You're stepping onto terrain you only half-know. This is where you need to be. There can be no discovery in a world where everything is known. A crucial part of the writing endeavor is the practice of remaining in the dark." "Discovery" would seem to imply a filling in or expansion of that half-knowledge he speaks of, and yet he seems also in favor of "remaining in the dark." There's a tension here that seems to derive from Boswell's sense that that half-known quality he speaks of is inherent not only in our work but also in the world. By these lights the half-known is fundamental to an ineffable sense of mystery in fiction, which in turn he sees as true to life: "A fully known world is devoid of mystery. . . . To make something fully known is to make it unreal." Existence in Boswell's formulation resists knowing, includes unknowing.

That's a fascinating and provocative assertion, with which I have great sympathy, but one that would seem to counter my own quest for knowledge in revision toward a "doneness" that resembles final understanding. It follows that a writer who only half-knows their world isn't yet done, needs to keep revising. One might say Boswell and I are in half-agreement. We start from a similar place, but diverge as to our destination. How to reconcile this contradiction? There are several possible arguments. Fiction after all isn't the "real," and indeed we value it for that very reason. Characters in fiction, it's often noted, can be more fully known than people in our own lives—wherein paradoxically lies the illusion of reality. Fiction, it's further claimed, frequently makes more sense than life, or indeed makes sense *of* life, which would suggest that part of fiction's role is to dispel mystery.

There may also be formal or genre considerations at play here. Short fiction frequently seeks to suggest or allude to something larger than itself—something it can't fully plumb in its brief scope. This is the notion of short fiction as the art of the glance, and the root of some readers' frustrations with its occasional opacity and elliptical nature.

For my part, I lean on a paradox from my physics days, the uncertainty principle, which suggests that we can never have complete knowledge of a system, that to know it—to observe it—is to alter it. I feel I can strive, in good faith, to know my own fiction (and thus myself) thoroughly, without ever quite dispelling that mystery of existence that Boswell so wisely intuits. The mystery seems intractable to me, impervious to my best efforts, even as I feel an artistic duty to assert those efforts. To put it another way—and this is an example I sometimes cite to students to clarify the distinction between vagueness (which they like to call ambiguity, but often reads as ambivalence) and mystery—my story "The Ugliest House in the World" turns on a tragic death. A young boy has been killed on a farm, crushed under a stone gatepost that he's been swinging from. The elderly neighbor who owns the gate feels guilty, even though he isn't responsible—the death is simply a tragic accident—and yet he still *feels* guilt (and our sympathies are with him because he feels it, because that feeling is what makes him human). So which is he—guilty or not guilty? Or somehow—despite their apparent mutual exclusivity—both? I think it's the latter, and that *bothness*—the logical irrationality of it and the simultaneous *emotional* rightness of it—is what I mean by an ineffable mystery.

But notice I haven't quoted from the story here. There's nothing artful in this bald exposition of the narrative, and yet even as plainly stated as this, the mystery gives me goosebumps. The mystery for me lies in the real world, in life, in human beings, not in the way the story has been written. The story doesn't create mystery or contrive it; the mystery seems inherent in the material and will remain mysterious however bluntly told. And yet, I had to write the story (and yes, revise it) in order to recognize that mystery. The more exactly we know something, the more its essential mystery asserts itself, just as the more exactly I measure a particle's position, the less I know of its momentum, a bit of anti-intuitive mystery that seems woven into the very fabric of reality.

Epilogue: Provincial Life Redux

Before I end, before I'm done, I want to return to my beginning, to my father, and that story told and retold in *The Welsh Girl* and elsewhere.

There are a lot of ways to revisit that story. I think of that Sikh teenager's reaction after the fight. His brief thanks, his shaking off of help, his hasty departure. As a child, I confess, I thought he was a little ungrateful—the scene of my father's heroism seemed to require something more. When I was older, when I wrote *The Welsh Girl*, it seemed to me he was a little ashamed, even embarrassed, the way any of us who take a fall on the ice will pick ourselves up quickly and move on, almost furtively, as if to deny what just happened. Lately, when I think of that story, I like to think he was being quintessentially British—stiff upper lip, no fuss please—the very thing those skinheads would have denied him (though in bleaker moments I also wonder if he just couldn't stand to see another white face, even a friendly one).

"Lately," of course, means in this moment, this temporal context, which over the course of the writing of this book has included stark political divisions in the UK (around Brexit) and in the US (following the 2016 election of Donald Trump).

In thinking and talking about some of those issues with students—many of them anxious and outraged—I've found myself reaching for one of the few things I can offer them: temporal perspective. I know it's been a solace to me. The night of the 2016 election I happened to be reading *March*, Congressman John Lewis's graphic memoir of the civil rights movement (I'd bought it originally for my son, who loved it). That narrative is framed by President Obama's inauguration in January 2009. We see the older John Lewis that morning getting ready to attend the ceremony and recalling his youth in the movement. It was heartbreaking to read on election night 2016, but also inspiring to see what Lewis and others had suffered and survived in the course of their civil rights work.

In a more modest, more personal way, in the closing weeks of 2016 I found myself reaching back to that story about my father—a white, working-class man coming to the aid of a person of color. And doing so at a time when Britishness very much meant whiteness, something that in the course of my lifetime, Brexit notwithstanding, has changed—a small note of hope.

I've talked earlier about the various revisions of this story and the shifts of context—to Nazi-era Germany, 1980s Detroit—in my fictional reimaginings of it, but this more recent telling in late 2016, faithful as I tried to make it, was also subject to contextual revision. That story meant something in the waning days of 2016 (and since, I'd warrant) that it didn't mean in 2005 when I was including it in *The Welsh Girl*, or even in 2014 when I was echoing it in *The Fortunes*. Even as I was trying to tell it more faithfully than before, to capture the past as memoir, the *present* was revising it.

There are other recent instances of this. The surge in sales of books like Orwell's *1984* (first published in 1949), or Sinclair Lewis's *It Can't Happen Here* (first published in 1935) or Margaret Atwood's *The Handmaid's Tale* (first published in 1985) after the election of Donald Trump, for example. Just a little further back in time the events of 9/11 revised the way the culture recalled Philippe Petit's tightrope walk between the Twin Towers in 1974, an instance of what Susan Sontag calls posthumous irony, deftly deployed by Colum McCann in his 2009 novel *Let the Great World Spin*. An example of something similar in popular culture would be the TV reboot of *Battlestar Galactica*, which took a creaky 1970s-era *Star Wars* knockoff—a kid-friendly space opera, basically—and re-tooled it as a thoughtful (if convoluted) allegory of the war on terror. The original series's initiating surprise attack has some echoes of Pearl Harbor, arguably, but the 2004 version plays as a mournful reimaging of 9/11 and its aftermath (including scenes of characters posting photos and names of the dead and missing on a wall). Further revisions to the premise—the enemy robots are now man-made, and have evolved into humanoids who can pass undetected among us—advance these ideas, but the *key* revision of meaning derives from the way the real world, rather than the fictional one, has changed.

Most recently, as I revise this book for publication, the world is grappling with the COVID-19 pandemic, and the way we apprehend old movies (*Contagion*, *Outbreak*), old songs ("It's the End of the World as We Know It"), and old books (*The Plague*, *Pale Horse*, *Pale Rider*, *The Decameron*) is being revised.

The most radical treatment of this kind of contextual revision in literature might be that of "Pierre Menard, Author of the Quixote" in Borges's famous story. The playfully paradoxical conceit is that Menard, a modern writer, is trying to rewrite Cervantes's *Don Quixote*—not copy it, nor revise it, but reproduce it word for word from his own imagination, a spontaneous act of both originality and plagiarism. Borges's narrator goes so far as to quote two identical passages and then extol their differences in deadpan fashion:

It is a revelation to compare Menard's *Don Quixote* with Cervantes'. The latter, for example, wrote (part one, chapter nine):

. . . truth, whose mother is history, rival of time, depository of deeds, witness of the past, exemplar and adviser to the present, and the future's counselor.

Written in the seventeenth century, written by the "lay genius" Cervantes, this enumeration is a mere rhetorical praise of history. Menard, on the other hand, writes:

> ... truth, whose mother is history, rival of time, depository of deeds, witness of the past, exemplar and adviser to the present, and the future's counselor.

History, the *mother* of truth: the idea is astounding. Menard, a contemporary of William James, does not define history as an inquiry into reality but as its origin. Historical truth, for him, is not what has happened; it is what we judge to have happened. The final phrases—*exemplar and adviser to the present, and the future's counselor*—are brazenly pragmatic.

The contrast in style is also vivid. The archaic style of Menard—quite foreign, after all—suffers from a certain affectation. Not so that of his forerunner, who handles with ease the current Spanish of his time.

As the narrator confoundingly concludes, "Cervantes' text and Menard's are verbally identical, but the second is almost infinitely richer." And perhaps here we find our purest revision, a draft in which not a single word has been changed, and yet which means differently.

This same revisionary force of time is even at play, albeit in more modest ways, on the anecdote about my father. I mentioned at the outset that the scene of that story, my hometown of Coventry, was the model for Eliot's *Middlemarch*. Yet the medieval city she would have known in the nineteenth century had been firebombed by the Luftwaffe in 1940, meaning that the street where I witnessed that neo-Nazi attack had been destroyed forty years earlier by "old" Nazis (the same Nazis who hound my character Rotheram from Germany in *The Welsh Girl*). The Coventry I grew up in had been *revised* since then—rebuilt in the postwar brutalist style—and begun like all revisions to forget itself, its literary heritage mostly commemorated in bathetic place names—the Middlemarch Business Park, the Middlemarch Ward of the local mental hospital, the George Eliot Secondary School (where my mother, a National Health dentist, would do visits). *My* Coventry is better captured by Philip Larkin's poem "I Remember, I Remember" (a title that sardonically references Thomas Hood's poem of happy childhood remembrance). Larkin also grew up in Coventry and the first stanza of his poem is engraved on a plaque at the modernist train station:

> Coming up England by a different line
> For once, early in the cold new year,
> We stopped, and, watching men with number plates
> Sprint down the platform to familiar gates,
> "Why, Coventry!" I exclaimed. "I was born here."

But it's his subsequent lines, not quoted on the plaque, that capture the town best:

> . . . A whistle went:
> Things moved. I sat back, staring at my boots.
> "Was that," my friend smiled, "where you 'have your
>   roots'?"
> No, only where my childhood was unspent . . .
>
> "You look as though you wished the place in Hell,"
> My friend said, "judging from your face." "Oh well,
> I suppose it's not the place's fault," I said.
>
> "Nothing, like something, happens anywhere."

Larkin, incidentally, would have had his own dark appreciation of Coventry's wartime history. During his childhood in the 1930s his father had been a Nazi sympathizer who'd attended Nuremberg rallies and displayed a statuette of Hitler on their mantelpiece.

Still, this old and much revisited story of my father and me has also come to my mind lately for other than political or literary reasons.

My father was still alive in 2016, but I realize that even then I occasionally spoke and wrote of him (in the first version of this essay delivered as a lecture at the Napa Valley Writers' Conference) in the past tense.

He was in a care home by then, suffering from dementia, his memory just about gone. Not an uncommon situation, and a distressing one for any of us. But a particular personal distress for me—and likely for any writer in such a situation—was that my father had often been a source of stories. Much of *The Welsh Girl* drew on his childhood wartime experiences in Wales. And by 2016 that source was stopped.

I'm sure his failing memory—the forgetting that is the final revision of many lives—prompted me to recall more of my memories of him. As did the fact that when I visited him in his home I often took my son, his grandson. My father did not often appear to remember me when we visited. He did respond to my boy, though, sometimes even mistaking him for me as a child. It means a lot to me that my son knew his grandfather—I never knew either of mine—and luckily for a few years at least in better health, but I also wonder sometimes how he will remember him.

What I know of my own grandfather, my father's father, is very limited. A few biographical facts (he was a slate quarry man with a small farm), a few foggy photos, and a handful of anecdotes, one of which, a story my father told about his father, I put in that story of mine "The Ugliest House in the World" in 1994:

> It's a story about the time my grandfather's dog had a big litter and he told the family that they were not to sell any of the pups. His brother disobeyed him and told him the dogs had died. When my grandfather found out he'd sold them he never spoke to him again as long as he lived. My father says his uncle was the one who met him at the station when he came back from his national service in Germany to see Grandfather before he died. Even then the old man wouldn't see his brother.

It occurred to me a while back that, with my father's memory fading (something the story itself—about a son and his aging, ailing father—anticipated), his mother dead, his eldest sister dead, and his surviving sister older than him, within the foreseeable future that story about my grandfather (plus a few memories of my older cousins) will be all that's left of him, in some sense.

Within a somewhat longer time frame—after I've died and my son is my age—the story I've been telling here about my father may similarly be all that's remembered of him. That's why I want to get it right.

Starting out as a writer, I used to think, as many of us do, that I wrote to defy death, in hope of posterity, which is to say immortality (a desire very easily deflected into a desire for fame). We write not to be forgotten. But the immortality I write for now, I realize, is less my own than that of those lost.

What fascinates me about this old story of that Coventry street is not me, my nonreaction. Perhaps I've worked through that in the intervening drafts. What fascinates me now is my father's reaction, why he—alone, among all the other adults on that street—stepped into the breach, and so swiftly, without apparent conscious decision making.

I used to think it had to do with his upbringing in Wales. He grew up in a small village where the habit of helping others was ingrained in him. Certainly he was always a good neighbor to folks on our street. One elderly woman across the road whom he used to look in on and do odd jobs for remembered him in her will by way of thanks—money that eventually went toward his own care.

So that's what I put it down to—a brand of rural, working-class, salt-of-the-earth decency (that as a middle-class city kid I never felt I had access to). But while all those things were true of my father, I've recently come to another conclusion, another understanding. One some of you—better readers of my life than I—may have already guessed.

When I began telling the story again in 2016, in this latest revision, it was informed by the times we live in, but also by my father's time of life, *and* my own. I was a father myself. I and my son were approximately the ages of my father and me in 1979.

As I mentioned earlier, my father was white and I'm mixed race, though those details were elided from the version of the story at the start of this book, and the version told in *The Welsh Girl* (even if Rotheram's German-Jewish status is a refraction of my dual identity). I don't think race—our races—factored much into my thinking when I was a child (he was just my dad, I was just his son) but I suspect it did feature in my father's. He was always very protective of me. I can recall being irritated at him for, say, stopping me going to a local park to play soccer with friends because a National Front march was taking place the same day.

Years afterward he told me he'd once found racist graffiti spray-painted on our garage door. The reason I only found out about it years later? He painted over it—his own act of revision—before I saw it. This man, I'm now sure, feared for me, his nonwhite son. And fear, among other things, is a great spur to the imagination—it keeps us up at night. It's blindingly obvious to me now that in his fear my father had imagined *me* as the victim of a racist attack. As a father myself, I now know what any of us would give to be able to defend our child in such a moment.

So here's how I now understand that moment, on that street, four decades ago, an understanding I've only discovered in the last couple of years (partly in the process of writing this very book). That poor Sikh teenager was the victim of the beating my father had always feared for me. My father was able to react so fast because he *recognized* instantly what he was seeing before his eyes, because he had already seen it in his nightmares, as if it were a prophecy. And for that reason, he was also ready to act.

To put it in more writerly terms: he had seen it in his (fearful) imagination; now he was re-seeing it in life. As a result, he was able to revise its outcome. (At least in this case. Tragically, his fears were not *only* imagined. Two years after his intervention on that street, another young Sikh man, twenty-year-old student Satnam Singh

Gill, was stabbed to death in broad daylight in the city center.)

There are lot of things the story might *mean* now. Political meanings about preparedness, about our ability to recognize evil before our eyes, about civic responsibility. I'm well aware, too, that the story might today be categorized as a white savior narrative. But none of these readings get to the personal meaning of the story, the reason I've felt compelled to retell it over and over.

For me, for all that I admired my father's heroism that day, there was always that glimmer of distance between us. He acted, I didn't (never mind *couldn't* or *shouldn't* as a child). That's the trace of shame, the fear that proud as I was of him, I might not grow into a man who would do the same, of whom he could be proud in turn, a fear that his warning to not get involved only stoked, as if he didn't think me strong enough.

But, of course, it's *not* a story of heroism or cowardice.

It's a story of love, of the *closeness* between us, not the distance. (Pride, it turns out, is how many men— fathers and sons, especially—*feel* love.[1])

And I'd suggest it's always been that story, even if it's taken me forty years to understand it. Forty years

---

1. A "darling" of an observation moved here from the novel I'm working on concurrently.

and countless retellings—in fiction, in anecdotes, in memory. Forty years of revision, essentially, to see what was there at the very beginning, at the heart of thing. Forty years to find the truth. And just in time (he passed away in the spring of 2018; the last time I told this story was at his funeral).

Forty years. And, you know what, it's worth it.

That's what revision is. And that's why we do it.

So is death the end of revision? It would, I suppose, fit the thesis that revision itself is a story, albeit there's something almost as dissatisfying about the notion as the idea of boredom as the end of revision. Both smack of entropy. But if revision is a story exhaling and inhaling, what else can it mean when the breathing stops? Perhaps our ultimate resistance to revision, to doneness is that it prefigures death—the final draft, the last word.[2] My father, it's true, is no longer making new stories, and the old ones about him are solidifying, stabilizing in their meanings. Still, maybe it's not death so much as repetition that ends revision. The more we retell it, the more a story hardens, thickens, sets. I no longer tear up when I tell this story as I first did.

And yet, new notes still emerge. My mother saying

---

2. *My* late epiphanic moment of doneness in the revision of *this* book—hence its title.

that my father several times intervened in similar fashion (of which I have no memory); she has her own story of her husband of over fifty years. Or that belated recall (for his eulogy) of my father buying me my first typewriter, the pair of us in a stationers, just down the street from the spot we saw that Sikh boy beaten. (Back then I aspired—as might be obvious by now—to be a sci-fi writer, another ending revised along the way.) That memory was especially meaningful to me, because I've often thought of myself becoming a writer despite my father, rather than because of him.

He was the one who encouraged me to study physics. He was an engineer himself, a telecoms engineer, as he put it. He met my mother when he was helping to install new telephone exchanges in Malaysia in the early 1960s. He never went to college, though. He learned his trade in the army—in a Royal Signals unit in Germany during his National Service in the 1950s—and then apprenticed with the General Electric Company, working for them until he retired in the 1980s. There was a watch to celebrate his twenty-five years with the company that I wore until the strap broke and I lost it (to my continuing heartbreak). Except he didn't retire. He was laid off in his late fifties, which to all intents and purposes amounted to retirement in that town, in that economy. It wasn't a surprise. He'd been expecting it, and dreading it, for more than a decade. Technical innovations—microchips, fiber optics—had rendered his expertise—vacuum tubes, electromechanical relays—obsolete. He wanted me to go to college and get a physics degree to avoid that fate, to understand the things that had passed him by. In that respect, my life was to be a new and improved version of his, a revision if you like. Perhaps not a perfection, but a refinement.

Of course, that's not the path I followed, and—though he tried to disguise it—I suspect he hated it when I became a writer, felt it as a kind of rejection. That was the version his resistance to revision took. He worried about my future, didn't understand the ambition—I don't recall ever seeing him read a novel—and expressed his confusion and concern at times by making me feel as if I was a disappointment to him. That sense likely colors the way I look back on that scene of his heroism and his later advice to not do the same. It felt in retrospect like another example of his lack of faith in me.

Sometimes people ask me what I remember of my science degree and I used to say, "Not much." That's true—most of the theorems and equations are lost to me now—but it was a more brutal assertion when I was younger. I felt I'd wasted three years of my life on physics. My father might have been disappointed in me, but I was resentful at the path he'd encouraged me to take.

Now, though, at a remove, it's possible to recognize the influence of those years on my habits of mind, my modes of thinking, and thus on my writing (as this book demonstrates).

And more than that, again with the advantage of hindsight, I suspect my eventual desire to be a writer and an academic may well owe something to a desire, bred of watching him, to not want to have a job, or an identity that could be taken away from me by a corporation. In that sense, I was, albeit unconsciously and certainly not according to his plans, revising his life.

It's sadly true, too, that this story isn't the whole of my father. It doesn't include his turn in later years toward a more conservative politics. But wouldn't we all want the stories that survive us to be the ones of us at our best?

The truth is that while our own ability to make new stories, and remake old ones, ends with us, life continues to revise us. Life in some sense *is* revision, and revision a measure of how alive a story continues to be.

Books Discussed and Consulted

Babel, Isaac. *The Complete Works*.

Borges, Jorge Luis. *Collected Fictions*.

Boswell, Robert. *The Half-Known World: On Writing Fiction*.

Carver, Raymond. *Beginners*.

Carver, Raymond. *Where I'm Calling From: Selected Stories*.

Chekhov, Anton. *The Selected Stories*.

Drnaso, Nick. *Sabrina*.

Hansen, Ron. *Nebraska*.

Hemingway, Ernest. *The Complete Short Stories*.

Joyce, James. *Dubliners*.

Kirschenbaum, Matthew G. *Track Changes: A Literary History of Word Processing*.

Lerner, Ben. *10:04*.

Machado, Carmen Maria. *Her Body and Other Parties*.

O'Connor, Flannery. *The Complete Stories*.

O'Connor, Frank. *Collected Stories*.

Percy, Benjamin. *Thrill Me: Essays on Fiction*.

Quade, Kirsten Valdez. *Night at the Fiestas.*

Tower, Wells. *Everything Ravaged, Everything Burned.*

Wershler-Henry, Darren. *The Iron Whim: A Fragmented History of Typewriting.*

Woodruff, Jay. *A Piece of Work: Five Writers Discuss Their Revisions.*

Acknowledgments

Thanks to Charles Baxter, Fiona McCrae, my wonderful editor Steve Woodward, and everyone at Graywolf Press; to my agent Maria Massie; to the Napa Valley Writers' Conference where I gave the talk that grew into this book; to Julie Orringer, Debra Spark, and Rebecca Scherm for pointing me toward valuable resources; to Kirstin Valdez Quade, Brit Bennett, and Carmen Maria Machado for so generously allowing me to discuss their examples of revision; and to all my colleagues and students down the years for sharing their work in progress and their insights into the revision process.

PETER HO DAVIES is the author of the novels *A Lie Someone Told You About Yourself*; *The Fortunes*, winner of the Anisfield-Wolf Award; and *The Welsh Girl*, longlisted for the Man Booker Prize, as well as two short story collections. His work has appeared in *Harper's*, the *Atlantic*, *Granta,* the *Paris Review*, the *Guardian*, the *New York Times*, and the *Washington Post*, and has been anthologized in *Prize Stories: The O. Henry Awards* and *Best American Short Stories.* Davies is also a recipient of fellowships from the Guggenheim Foundation and the National Endowment for the Arts, and is a winner of the PEN/Malamud and PEN/Macmillan Awards. Born in Britain to Welsh and Chinese parents, he has taught at the University of Oregon, Emory University, Northwestern University, and, for the past twenty years, in the Helen Zell Writers' Program in creative writing at the University of Michigan in Ann Arbor.

The text of *The Art of Revision: The Last Word* is set in Warnock Pro, a typeface designed by Robert Slimbach for Adobe Systems in 2000. Book design by Wendy Holdman. Composition by Bookmobile Design and Digital Publisher Services, Minneapolis, Minnesota. Manufactured by Versa Press on acid-free, 30 percent postconsumer wastepaper.